OUR EARTH CRIES OUT

Early Naturalist's Warnings, Present Environmental Degradation, and A Crisis in Body, Mind, and Spirit

Dr. Laren R. Winter

This book is dedicated to my best friend and wife, Karen, who helped me edit and organize the content of this book through many revisions. She is also my partner in environmental concerns, awareness, and love of nature.

Alienation from the world of nature has led us to extravagant expectations concerning the benefits of our modern technologies. These expectations have blinded us to the evils inherent in the very solutions to life's difficulties we were proposing. By using chemical fertilizers, we increased our grain harvest but destroyed the natural fertility of the soil. Because of our clear-cut assault on the woodlands, the forests can no longer renew themselves. In relentlessly pursuing marine life, we depleted the abundance that was there for millennia.

In the last two centuries, as we have become more proficient in manipulating the nonhuman components of the Earth community, we have become progressively alienated from the most elementary awareness of our role and place in that community. We expected the entire universe to respond to us, the human component, as the ultimate reference and arbiter of value. Frustrated when we realize that we do not have control over the world around us, we sink into a deepening cultural impasse.

In becoming a commerce-dependent consumer society, we have ignored the essential elements and ideals necessary to sustain any viable human community. For example, by enclosing ourselves in automobiles, we have isolated people from one another and destroyed a certain sense of community. Moreover, we find that the distance between the affluent and the less well-off and from the impoverished is constantly increasing. We are isolated and alienated, both as individuals and as communities. We are held together mainly by the political legal binding of the modern nationalist state and by our dependence on an industrial, commercial, consumer society.

Thomas Berry, The Sacred Universe.

TABLE OF CONTENTS

AWAKENING

The history of the United States is the story of humankind living with, being fed from, and struggling to dominate the natural world. America's story has been a remarkable story of people and the land, forests, plains, water, and all its natural resources. It has been the story of a natural heritage that is varied and extremely interesting filled with new discoveries about the land, exciting outdoor adventures, and the continual will to survive in difficult natural environments. American institutions and American values have developed and been shaped by the history toward nature. It has been equally the story of America's lack of stewardship in seizing, using, squandering and, belatedly protecting and developing that heritage. Presently, environmental degradation continues at a rapid pace. The extensive list of how our natural world is being destroyed is not unlike what the early naturalists warned us about not so long ago. Much is being done to protect the environmental and America can be proud of its successes. The present-day issues are so massive and interconnected that without major changes in our commitment to not only saving the environment but also saving ourselves the result will be catastrophic. Ultimately, it is also the story of sabotaging our spiritual, emotional, and physical health because of our lack of looking beyond our present selves.

From the beginning Americans had a serious awareness of the land and the wilderness. Most Americans have always saluted the incredible bounty of nature but at the same time abused and abandoned it. John James Audubon began to stir the conscience of America, but not until the time of John Wesley Powell, in the late 1800's, did we begin to understand that our resources were not inexhaustible. The Native Americans and these few individuals called naturalists have been the prime movers from the past in trying to preserve the beauty of the land, interpret its past, present, and future, and tell of the enjoyment of being with nature. Only during the twentieth century did the United States really begun to listen to the words of those men and women who fought for environmental awareness in America. It is true that well into the twenty-first century citizens of the United States have carried the message of the naturalists into action for protecting and saving the environment. It is also true that saving the environment is a battle against greed, big corporate power, and politicians who are unwilling to make difficult decisions that require them to commit to pushing back against those who have no vision of the future beyond getting reelected.

In order to understand how America developed an environmental consciousness it is necessary to consider what was written by or about naturalists who were significant leaders in helping shape America's understanding of the environment. The words of naturalists who have played the major roles in these events tell the story and their part in it. Prominent naturalists from our past who have heavily influenced our environmental awareness today are: John James Audubon, Henry David Thoreau, John Wesley Powell, John Muir, Gifford Pinchot, Enos Mills, Aldo Leopold, and Rachel Louise Carson.

Over the centuries of our country the men and women who gifted us with so much knowledge about our environment and who worked tirelessly to save it for future generations have been called preservationists, conservationists, environmentalists, ecologists, visionaries, and naturalists. These are individuals who communicate meanings and relationships of the environment through creative writing, interpreting, or legislation for the purpose of the betterment of humans and the preservation of the development of the land for the future of all living beings. They have advocated for preserving, protecting, and maintaining natural resources in their original state. They have also shown us that careful management and enlightened use of natural resources is the only way to insure a future of sufficiency for all humans.

John James Audubon became a full-time ornithologist and naturalist after several bad business ventures. Audubon painted birds and studied their environment. Audubon's life was with nature and he wanted to share the emotions and beauty surrounding each inhabitant. He wanted the beauty of the wilderness to be left undisturbed and the destruction of the environment stopped. Audubon wanted his work to rekindle a stewardship of the land.

Henry David Thoreau's life was part spiritual quest and part experiential living in its simplest form. His writings were models for cultural and social issues of the time. He modeled simple living by experiencing a two year stay at Walden Pond. Exploring the natural history of his environment was a daily adventure into nature. Thoreau believed most of the comforts of life were not necessary and usually were hindrances to living a more meaningful life.

John Wesley Powell studied science at every opportunity. He led the first two expeditions of the Colorado River and studied the arid land of the West. As the father of the United States Geological Survey he pushed for new land and water use control in the West. Powell gave to America a scientific understanding of the land and how to work with it.

John Muir grew into adulthood wildly excited about the wonders of nature. He wandered throughout America studying the wilderness areas. Muir, considered the father of the National Park Service, pushed for preservation of all wilderness areas. His writings have given America hope for the wilderness as a place to go in search of a vision.

Gifford Pinchot became the father of the National Forest Service after studying silviculture in France. He worked with Theodore Roosevelt in introducing the issue of conservation into politics. Pinchot believed the forests should be a workshop for man and instituted the multiple-use concept of wilderness areas.

Enos Mills moved to Longs Peak, Colorado, as a young man. He began a guide service and became known for his guiding and writing ability. Mills helped establish many national parks and was a major figure in the establishment of the National Park Service. Mills, a preservationist, wanted the wilderness to be available to future generations.

Aldo Leopold, the father of wildlife management, worked for the National Forest Service and was a college professor. He believed people should be partners with the land and not conquerors. Leopold wanted a land ethic developed in people thereby enabling them to live in harmony with the land. His scientific approach to viewing the environment has furthered America's awareness for all things natural.

Rachel Louise Carson was a conservationist and a marine biologist and only the second woman to be hired full-time with the United States Bureau of Fisheries. Her research unexpectedly led her to the role of pesticides causing environmental crisis in all living things. Carson's tireless push to ban chemical pesticides led to a policy of banning DDT and other pesticides at the national level. Carson foretold the extreme health consequences on humanity and all the natural world that would transpire as weakened environmental systems were impacted by the use of poisonous chemicals. The Environmental Defense Fund was created in 1967 largely because of Carson's research and writings.

Muir, Mills, and Thoreau were called preservationists as they wanted to preserve all things in their natural condition. Audubon, Powell, Pinchot, Leopold, and Carson were called conservationists because they believed the environment was available to be used for various things but must also be protected from overuse. Powell, Carson, and Leopold studied the land scientifically. Muir, Mills, Thoreau, and Audubon viewed the land from an aesthetic viewpoint. Pinchot saw the environment as a workshop for humankind. All eight naturalists contributed to a better understanding and awareness of the environment. Each naturalist had a unique life style, lived specific environmental beliefs, and contributed greatly to the future of saving and healing our natural environment of today.

However, despite these centuries of the Naturalist voices advocating for saving our earth, development of a lived environmental ethic and consciousness still proceeds slowly. Progress still consists largely of individuals and groups who see the impact of environmental destruction on all life forms who push against ridged and powerful interests who want to control and dominate the natural world. It is postulated that the solution to this dilemma is more quality education, both in content and focus, for men and women of every age, not simply education in quantity as has been done in the past. Mainly the content should be education in voluntary stewardship, voting for persons who are concerned with environmental issues, joining supportive organizations, and respecting the land. However, no important change in ethics will be accomplished without change in intellectual emphasis, loyalties, affections, convictions and commitments to the environment. The importance of being knowledgeable of environmental principles is simply this: How we treat our environment will determine our future.

Despite the voices of concern from our early naturalists the degradation of the environment has continued at an alarming rate. The changes and challenges the early naturalists presented us continue to be extremely relevant to the environmental issues we face today. Progress has been made in many areas and an environmental ethic is lived by numerous individuals and groups. Unfortunately, the unstoppable growth of the country has caused an overwhelming number of environmental issues to push us to the point of no return in saving the environment. Population explosion has caused more pollution, more land use, more need for clean water, more food, and the desire for more technology which American's seem to believe will save them. The overall result is more climate change and global warming. Without extreme changes in solving these issues more severe human health problems will continue at massive levels.

Extreme environmental damage also damages humanity in body, mind, and spirit. Just as ecosystems are ravaged so are the humans who share the natural world with all other living species. Physically humanity seems to be in better health than ever. However, sheer numbers of humans show that for all the progress that is alleged in the physical condition of humankind there are continually more health issues and risks.

Emotionally humankind's mental health is suffering as a result of environmental sickness. Anxiety, depression, anger, and severe stress have all grown in extreme ways. More pills are offered to ease the mental trauma. More growth of cities and suburbs has pushed humanity into a personal space crisis. Nature is pushed further away and emotional re-creation through the sharing of the beauty of creation is less possible. Humankind often lives in automobiles and large buildings cut off from the healing experience of nature. The desire for emotional wellness is discussed and sought after more than ever before, but is often only experienced through pictures, words in a book or other technological means and not in reality.

As humans struggle to maintain healthy bodies and healthy minds humankind is also pushed into a spiritual crisis. When physical and emotional health have deteriorated an even more serious crisis occurs in the spiritual wellness, which is the third part of the human trinity. It is more difficult to find a peaceful and serene center to life today. Many world religions are clear that there is a relationship between a healthy natural world and the spiritual center of humankind. The continual search for the meaning of existence has been the sacred journey of humanity since the beginning of history. Early humankind lived, survived and died within nature. The connection was strong because all of creation shared it together. Beliefs were developed that explained the relationship. The environment was revered and worshiped. As the present became history in the continual movement of time the ever-evolving cycle changed humanity. It separated itself from nature and the sacred relationship. The spiritual connection lessened and wasn't as needed as it was before when humanity and nature co-existed. Humanity is now embraced by a spiritual crisis and is losing the environmental marriage of the life-giving human spirit and a life of peace.

The early naturalists left us the gift and the roadmap of the need for a healthy environment to save ourselves from destruction. Humanity has pushed, used, abused, violated, and overwhelmed our natural world. Words of the naturalists are often relegated to dusty bookshelves. Humankind suffers in body, mind and spirit and our earth cries out in pain.

PART I

NATURALIST'S VOICES FROM THE PAST

With concern and vision for America's future many figures from history gave their lives to developing a land ethic and future view of the natural world. They were fierce advocates for the protection of nature so as to combat the careless approaches to nature that were becoming more prevalent. These individuals from America's past were given the title of "naturalist" because of their expert views on the natural world of all living beings. They communicated how to understand the value of having a relationship with the environment through creative writing, interpreting, and legislation for the purpose of the betterment of humankind. The naturalists' purpose was the preservation and development of the land for the future of humanity.

In the search to understand how America began to develop an environmental ethic for sharing the natural world for future generations it is important to remember what these men and women of history actually gave to America and the world. Their writings, speeches, and lifestyles gave their stories through individual environmental beliefs, and their contributions to environmental awareness.

A review of each naturalist's written material before, during, and after significant events demonstrates how those critical events helped shape an environmental ethic for the future. The events included: action on the preservation of wildlife; identification of flora and fauna in many parts of the United States; the Reclamation Act; a conservation plan for the settlement of arid country; a program of water rights; a development of the ecology of the plains and high plateaus; the exploration of the Colorado River; the establishment of the National Geological Survey; the establishment of the Sierra Club; the establishment of many National Parks including Sequoia, Yosemite, Mount Rainer, Crater Lake, Glacier, Mesa Verde, Grand Canyon, Rocky Mountain and Olympic National Parks; game preserves; the term "conservation" and the conservation movement; watersheds; establishment of the National Forest Service; the National Park Service; wildlife, and wilderness problems; establishment of Wilderness areas; the National Audubon Society; the Pinchot Institute; national ban on DDT and other pesticides; awareness of our coastal sea areas; and the Environmental Defense Fund.

The naturalists were courageous trailblazers with visionary approaches and were fellow travelers with all living beings on the planet. They showed us that each life form needs all the other life forms in order to survive. Humanity exists by cooperation and sharing according to the naturalists. An environmental conscience tells us that humankind must offer the same cooperation, sharing, and generosity to all life forms. Humanity exists to use its abilities to communicate, observe, research, and reason to co-exist with all of creation. The path less traveled is the one of thriving in relationship with the earth. The other path, the one humanity is on now, is the one with no relationship with creation and the brutal domination of the earth leading to more and more difficulties of sheer survival.

JOHN JAMES AUDUBON, 1785-1851

A Voice for Nature

"A true conservationist is a man who knows that the world is not given by his fathers, but borrowed from his children." John James Audubon

John James Audubon was born to Jean Audubon and Mademoiselle Rabin in La Rochelle, France, 1785. After the death of his natural mother, John James was raised by his father and his second wife Anne Moynet. John James was very much influenced by his parents because of their great interest in the outdoors and their love for art and the capturing of nature's beauty.

Audubon's traits in his childhood were very appropriate for his eventual chosen career. As a child he spent his time in the surrounding woods or reading books about the wilds of the world. He had an intimacy with the wilds which would accompany his steps throughout his life. With advancing years "his determination to know nature" increased almost to an obsession. Audubon, even as a young child, longed to understand nature and the innate powers by which the spells of its enchantment came about. In order to understand nature, he felt he must ally himself with nature and devote himself to it. He was inspired with an ardent desire to understand the productions of nature.

The creative impulse of wanting to capture nature with all its splendor haunted Audubon as a child. Audubon's father taught him to look at birds and recognize the emotions of the experience because all persons must look up to the birds and with that, the heavens.

As a child he complained to his father that he could not get close enough to the birds in the trees. His father, opening a book and pointing to an illustration of a bird, told him he could see birds more closely in books. With that, Audubon said he would draw his own pictures with the crayons his folks had given him for his birthday. Thus, reproducing the beautiful objects of the material world, mirrored by his imagination, arrested his desire to possess the productions of nature. To be free, to be true, to follow a bird in the woods or an impulse with his pencil, these were the things that gave meaning to his life. "My pencil gave birth to a family of cripples" said Audubon.

Audubon lived in an age when the worthy pioneers were slaying passenger pigeons by the thousands and burning forests so as to remake the land into a likeness of their mother countries. After moving to America as a young man, Audubon continued his research. Difficulty, toil, privation, and danger often attended his research throughout the entire American territory. It was Audubon's custom to travel alone with the elements and wild animals. From daylight to nightfall he would roam furnished only with his inner strength and gun in order to bring back new bird specimens, put them in lifelike attitudes with wire, and then bring to life on paper with imagination and pencil. Because of the destruction going on across the continent, Audubon's subconscious expedient mission seemed to be to draw most of the birds of America before it was too late.

Audubon was a wonderful painter and a charming fellow but in business affairs a failure. After his marriage to Lucy Blakewell, Audubon tried his luck in several business ventures, but they always seemed to go badly for him. Mainly because when important engagements to consider business problems came due, he made the excuse of having to get specimens for some zoologist or ornithologist. Audubon continually betrayed his responsibility to business because of its monotony and confusion. He chose instead to draw birds and searched the skies and shorelines for birds no matter what kind of weather. One account of Audubon the businessman tells how he let his horse stray with a saddlebag of cash while he pursued an unfamiliar warbler into the canebrake. Although luck was with him, it was no wonder that people suspected him of being more a dreamer than a man of commerce. Wherever he traveled he studied birds and voiced curiosity about every aspect of outdoor life. Luckily for Audubon his wife and family shared his zest for life, which for them was coming closer to nature.

Audubon's knowledge of people in no way equaled his growing knowledge of wildlife. After being taken advantage of on several occasions he ended up in bankruptcy and lost almost everything. Pursuant to his business failures he became a full-time artist-ornithologist and even though existence was at times painful, he was finally doing exactly what he wanted.

Even though his first love was painting birds, many times, because of lack of money, he had to become a commercial painter. Audubon had many jobs teaching painting and drawing to rich people's kids. As usual, he most always was negatively exploited. It was a chance meeting with Alexander Wilson, the father of American ornithology that turned Audubon's life in the direction it was to go. Even after Audubon departed from business and began his efforts to publish his bird drawings, success was not always with him. Audubon's personal account of one unlucky incident reflects his sometimes backward spiral.

"An accident to two hundred of my original drawings nearly put a stop to my researches in ornithology," said Audubon. "Once, before proceeding to Philadelphia on business, I placed all my drawings in the care of a relative for several months. On my return I asked for my box and what I was pleased to call my treasure. It was produced and opened. But, a pair of Norway rats had taken possession, and reared a young family among the gnawed bits of paper which, a few months before, had represented nearly a thousand inhabitants of the air. The burning that rushed through my brain was too great to be endured, affecting the whole of my nervous system. I slept not for several nights, and the days passed like days of oblivion until the animal powers were recalled into action through the strength of my constitution. I took up my gun, my notebook, and pencil, and went forth into the woods as gaily as if nothing had happened. I felt pleased that I might now make much better drawings than before. Before three years had elapsed I had filled my portfolio again."

The above account describes the deep emotions Audubon felt for his work. On another occasion his stored drawings were once again damaged by an explosion of gunpowder. But, he was determined to draw most every bird in America so on he trudged.

Audubon continually ventured into the deep forests to study wildlife and find new specimens. He broke barriers with the Indians by drawing pictures of birds and animals familiar to them. He demonstrated his marksmanship for the Indians by shooting between the gleaming eyes of wolves that skulked in the shadows near the campfire. Audubon's ability to relate to those close to nature also included the animals of the forest. Many animals seemed to sense friendliness and mission. On one occasion, Audubon, carried a female broadwinged hawk from a tree beneath a kerchief. Audubon perched her on a stick at his drawing table where she offered no resistance as he smoothed her ruffled feathers. After drawing the hawk which remained immobile on a perch during the drawing, Audubon launched her out the window where she flew off without a sound or outcry. Many birds trusted Audubon to the point that he could hold them in his hand and study them.

Audubon's desire to publish works on the birds of America and the reward of each was a task in which he encountered almost insurmountable odds. On many occasions, while showing his work in America, dissenters refused to even consider purchasing his drawings because of his lack of a classical education. Audubon stated that the accuracy of his drawing, based as it was on keen observation, made up for his academic deficiencies. This usually fell on closed ears. Also, Audubon was shunned because he was only a field naturalist and not a scientific one. The scientific naturalists claimed that Audubon could shoot a bird, preserve it, and make it live again but he could not describe it in scientific, perfectly intelligible terms and that, to them, was the most important aspect of this type of work. Sadly, Audubon found he must travel to England and France to gain the recognition he deserved.

Audubon reached a turning point in his lonely, beleaguered career on November 20, 1826 when a text of his ornithological observations was published as *Ornithological Biography*. Soon after this, and during his many art showings, people in England and France began to subscribe to his *Birds of America* collection. During this time Audubon was inducted into nineteen honor societies. Even though recognition was finally coming to Audubon, progress was still slow. After running into many barriers Audubon protested to one dignitary.

"So much remains to be done," said Audubon, "that it is now with a sore heart that I must relinquish the ardent wish I had, to see, before my death, the natural history of that fine country fairly investigated. Many besides yourself expected my work would fall through, but I have industry, perseverance, and honesty on my side." Audubon's hope was that science, through his feeble efforts, would advance one step in its progress.

After returning to America, and, finally achieving recognition, Audubon finished his third and final volume of *The Birds of America*. A larger *Ornithological Biography* and *Synopsis of The Birds of America* were also completed. Audubon then began his work on *Quadrupeds* because he stated that unless he did so, no one else would for years to come and he knew it was badly needed. *The Birds of America* consists of three volumes of birds painted by Audubon showing the type of environment in which they live. The *Ornithological Biography* describes the characteristics and habits of each of the paintings in Audubon's *Birds* volumes. Audubon's *Synopsis of the Birds of America* summarizes the *Birds* volumes with the *Ornithological Biography*. *Quadrupeds* is Audubon's paintings and observations of many of America's four-legged animals. As his work progressed, he was always eager to tell of his work and ability. He told Daniel Webster, the Secretary of State, that there should be a new National Museum of Natural History and he should be the head.

Audubon's work has contributed to and understanding of the beauty and awareness of nature in many ways. His written and published works have awakened the natural instincts of the woodsman in humans and, therefore, an awareness for the environment. Audubon's personal diaries are the most valuable in understanding his awareness and aesthetic feelings of being with the environment. A reader of Audubon becomes more in touch with the environment and the importance of preserving what natural environment we have left.

John James Audubon's life was the natural world. It was his love for nature which he wanted to share with the world. Audubon's goal was not to just paint nature's inhabitants but to share the emotions and beauty which surrounded each inhabitant. It was only by understanding these surroundings that people could appreciate the intricate pattern by which the universe is formed and, therefore, comprehend the necessity of maintaining the balance of nature. This maintenance of the balance of nature was the underlying principle behind Audubon's work, which he hoped to impress on people through his drawings and bibliography of each drawing. There was an extreme urgency in Audubon's work because he felt the natural history of America must be recorded before it vanished forever. He seemed to foresee the future of the land and the painful lessons which America would have to learn.

Many times during Audubon's ventures into America's backcountry he encountered the very destruction of the land and its inhabitants which made his work that much more urgent and which also sorrowed him to deep despair. Audubon's own accounts of two of these incidents show how distraught he became.

Audubon wrote,

"The name 'eggers' is given those who make a business of collecting eggs of wild birds for distant markets. Their object is to plunder every nest they can find, no matter, where or at what risk. These pests often brutally destroy the poor creatures, once they have robbed them. I could not believe all their cruelties which gave me no little horror. After one day of killing birds for a barbeque and trampling chicks within the shell the eggers revisit every spot to collect the eggs laid since their departure and to shoot as many more birds as they need. At every step the egger picks up an egg so beautiful that that one might think that a man with any feeling would pause to consider his motive for carrying it off. But nothing of the sort occurs to him. Dollars alone clink in his mind. This war of extermination cannot last many more years. In less than half a century the wonderful nurseries will be entirely destroyed, unless some kind of governmental action will stop the shameful destruction."

During Audubon's travels in the west he related his feelings concerning the buffalo of the Great Plains.

"One can hardly conceive how it happens that so many buffalo are still to be found, regardless of the number that die and are murdered daily on those boundless wastes called prairies. But, before many years the buffalo will have disappeared. Surely this will not be allowed to happen. What a terrible destruction of life, and for nothing or next to it. The tongues are brought in. The flesh is left to wolves and birds of prey, or to rot where these fine animals fell. The prairies are covered with the skulls of the victims."

Audubon's words fell on mute ears for nearly forty years. The dream Audubon had, to see the natural history of the country fairly well investigated before his death, was only partially achieved. But, his efforts advanced science tremendously after his death.

During Audubon's lifetime he witnessed the disappearance of many of the forests and their animals. On one of Audubon's adventures he wrote in his diary, "Where much longer can man find the beauty of the wilderness undisturbed? The wanton destruction of the environment must be stopped and controlled." With every act of environmental destruction Audubon witnessed, his investigations into the natural history of America increased with a frenzy.

Audubon's belief about protecting the natural environment can be stated briefly. He believed America must save the wilderness and its inhabitants for future generations in order to develop emotional ties. Audubon was a very realistic individual. He knew experiencing nature might soon depend on his work so his life was devoted to that end.

Through his work John James Audubon helped people rekindle their dreams and realize their stewardship of the land. Humankind is not and cannot be separated from the environment. Through personal involvement with the beauty, mystery, and tranquility of the land an individual can develop awareness, feeling, and perspective. Audubon lived this, taught this, and recorded this, so individuals could have reverence for humanity through reverence with nature.

The National Audubon Society, headquartered in New York City, was founded for the express purpose of carrying on John James Audubon's work and beliefs about caring for the environment. Through the large organizational structure of the National Audubon Society a multitude of individuals become aware of present-day environmental concerns. One way the Society affects society is through various centers.

Audubon Centers are outdoor areas utilized for teaching environmental care. Each center is unique in natural landscape with trails through diversified habitats. These areas are designed to open the eyes of young and old to the natural world about them, develop interest and enthusiasm to learn more, and motivate a sense of responsibility to help maintain a healthy environment. An interpretive building at each center houses attractive ecological displays and offers a service department featuring inexpensive conservation resource material helpful to teachers and others. The chief goal of the Centers is not instruction but provocation.

The National Audubon Society also offers a Naturalist Training Program. The training program is an intensive thirteen-week on-the-job training experience designed to familiarize college students, graduates or other adults with all facets of nature center work. The training takes place at several of the Audubon Centers.

Many Audubon workshops are also offered throughout the United States. The purpose of the Audubon workshops is to add to one's knowledge and understanding of the natural world thereby developing both an appreciation and an affection for nature and all its processes including a sense of individual responsibility for the care and wise use of our natural resources. The Audubon workshops are open to all people and may be taken for university credit.

The National Audubon Society has also developed Outdoor Exploration Programs for school and youth groups, weekend and summer nature discovery programs for selected age groups, and ecologically-oriented curricula for classes in school districts, teacher education workshops, and counselor training programs.

Throughout Audubon's life he gave everything he had for the most beautiful things he could see, not just the birds he painted, but all of life. Audubon's life was nature. Life was holy ground for John James Audubon. He walked carefully in nature, venturing courageously on unbroken trails, missing no birds in the bushes, exulting in the gift of life itself, and pressing it on as a creator to others. Audubon wanted to draw birds for all to remember and he devoted his life to that goal. It was only after his death in 1851 that Audubon became recognized for his work

John James Audubon, the naturalist, has gifted the world on the beauty of nature in a way almost unparalleled by any individual in America's history. His words have opened the nation's eyes to the conservation and appreciation of wildlife, wilderness, natural resources, and natural beauty

HENRY DAVID THOREAU: 1817-1862

Early Whispers

"In society you will not find health, but in nature. Unless our feet at least stood in the midst of nature, all our faces would be pale and livid. Society is always diseased, and the best is the most so. There is no scent in it so wholesome as that of the pines, nor any fragrance so penetrating and restorative as the life-everlasting in high pastures. I would keep some book of natural history always by me as a sort of elixir, the reading of which should restore the tone of the system. To the sick, indeed, nature is sick, but to the well, a fountain of health. To him who contemplates a trait of natural beauty no harm nor disappointment can come. The doctrines of despair, of spiritual or political tyranny or servitude, were never taught by such as shared the serenity of nature." Henry David Thoreau

David Henry Thoreau was born in Concord, Massachusetts, in 1817. His father, John Thoreau was a pencil maker and his mother Cynthia Dunbar Thoreau was a homemaker. He was the last male descendant of a French ancestor who came to the new country from the Isle of Guernsey. After graduating from Harvard College in 1837 he reversed his names and became Henry David Thoreau.

For a few weeks Thoreau was on the faculty of Concord Public Schools but because of his strong views against corporal punishment he resigned. The result was that from 1834-41 Thoreau ran a private school named the Concord Academy with his brother John. Lockjaw claimed John in death in 1842 and for a long period of time following John's death Thoreau's life was greatly impacted. The two brothers were extremely close and had traveled extensively together. In later writings Thoreau shared many of their adventures and sojourns into nature.

The main professions of that time were law, church, business, and medicine. Against the advice of family and friends Thoreau made the decision that he wasn't interested in any of these professions. His life choices at that time led him to natural history, nature, and the human condition. He began journaling on October 22, 1837, at the urging of Ralph Waldo Emerson.

Emerson, Thoreau's early mentor, was a Transcendentalist philosopher. Emerson, and the Transcendentalists believed that an ideal spiritual state transcends a person's physical and empirical life. A person achieves insight by personal intuition rather than religious doctrine according to the Transcendentalists. Emerson taught Thoreau that nature was the outward sign of a person's inward spirit expressing the radical correspondence of visible things and human thoughts. That teaching included the message that human institutions were corrupt and misleading and that the personal God of Christians was mythical and remote. As a result, there was only one place in the world to receive order, morality, the good, and the beautiful and that was nature. It was only in nature that the divine expressed itself directly to a person's soul. These early teachings to Thoreau were the beginning of a life in nature.

In 1837 Thoreau gave a commencement address at his alma mater, Harvard. In it he expanded on Ralph Waldo Emerson's *Nature*. Thoreau stated that six days out of the week should be for feeding our soul with "sublime revelations of nature."

Thoreau moved into the William Emerson, brother of Ralph Waldo, house on April 18, 1841. Thoreau tutored the Emerson sons on Staten Island. In July 1848 Thoreau left the Emerson home and eventually moved to a Concord home. There he worked in his family's pencil factory which he did for most of his adult life. During this time Henry, applying himself diligently to making pencils, believed he could make better pencils than were available. He experimented and worked with chemists and artists in new designs for pencils. When he was congratulated by friends and told he would now make a fortune he replied that he would never make another pencil. "Why should I," said Thoreau, "I would not do again what I have done once." He then resumed his natural history and nature studies.

Over the years Thoreau payed off his financial debts by living in the Emerson house helping with the household. During this time he worked on his manuscript, *Walden, or Life in the Woods*, which he published in 1854. It was his writing about his two years, two months, and two days at Walden

Pond. This was part spiritual quest and part personal memoir. His writings were models for cultural and social issues of the time.

The years of 1845 through 1849 are often called the Civil Disobedience and Walden years in Thoreau's life. A man named Ellery Channing, in 1845, told Thoreau to, "Go out upon the land and build yourself a hut and there begin the grand process of devouring yourself alive. I see no other alternative, no other hope for you." In two months, Thoreau began his experiment of simple living over a two-year period of time. He moved into his hut that he built on the land owned by Emerson. His hut was at Walden Pond.

The Civil Disobedience part of Thoreau's life involved Sam Staples, the local tax collector. Staples met Thoreau around July 24, 1846. Staples asked Thoreau to pay six years of delinquent poll taxes. Thoreau, because of his opposition to the Mexican-American War and slavery, refused to pay. He spent a night in jail. From that night in jail Thoreau lectured before the Concord Lyceum on the relation of the individual to the State. And the rights of the individual to self-government. Thoreau put his lecture into an essay entitled "Resistance to Civil Government".

In explanation of his time at Walden Pond Thoreau said,

"I went to the woods because I wished to live deliberately, to front only the essential facts of life, and see if I could not learn what it had to teach, and not, when I came to die, discover that I had not lived. I did not wish to live what was not life, living is so dear; nor did I wish to practice resignation unless it was quite necessary. I wanted to live deep and suck out all the marrow of life, to live sturdily and Spartan-like as to put to rout all that was not life, to cut a broad swath and shave close to drive life into a corner, and reduce it to its lowest terms, and if it proved to be mean, why then to get the whole and genuine meanness of it, and publish its meanness to the world; or if it were sublime, to know it by experience, and be able to give a true account of it in my next excursion."

The exploration of natural history of his area was part of Thoreau's journey through life. He studied botany and made observations in his journal. He observed Concord's natural area and wrote about how fruit ripened over time, bird's migration, and how the water in Walden Pond changed. He also spent time as a land surveyor and studied natural history of the twenty-six square miles in which he resided. Thoreau filled several notebooks with his observations about nature and the natural history of his area. He also read extensively about the lives of Lewis and Clark, James Cook, David Livingstone, and various artic explorers and absorbed that knowledge into his own sojourns into nature.

Thoreau also studied Charles Darwin's *On the Origin of Species* and was a believer of the theory of evolution by natural selection. "The development theory implies a greater vital force in Nature because it is more flexible and accommodating, and equivalent to a sort of constant new creation."

As an elegy to his brother, John, Thoreau wrote, *A Week on the Concord and Merrimack Rivers,* about their 1839 trip to the White Mountains.

> *"The natural historian is not a fisherman, who prays for cloudy days and good luck merely, but as fishing has been styled "a contemplative man's recreation," introducing him profitably to woods and water, so the fruit of the naturalist's observations is not in new genera or species, but in new contemplations still, and science is only a more contemplative man's recreation. The seeds of the life of fishes are everywhere disseminated, whether the winds waft them, or the waters float them, or the deep earth holds them; wherever a pond is dug, straightway it is stocked with this vivacious race. They have a lease of nature, and it is not yet out."*

Henry David Thoreau said, "Most of the luxuries and many of the so-called comforts of life are not only not indispensable, but positive hindrances to the elevation." His writings on nature and human existence were statements about the interconnectedness of life. He advocated recreational hiking and water activities and preserving natural areas. He also was outspoken about saving wilderness areas as places all people could visit.

Some called Thoreau an ascetic. He mostly ate vegetables, ate little meat, drank only water, and he never married. Although, there did seem to be one lady who wanted to marry him. Henry said the one-sided relationship was very tragic. His behavior suggested he went into nature to save his soul an only in nature could be find salvation. Henry said, "I do believe in simplicity. When the mathematician would solve a difficult problem, he first frees the equation from all encumbrances, and reduces it to its simplest terms. So simplify the problem of life, distinguish the necessary and the real."

Blending of both nature and culture was the "pastoral" world for him. Wild areas were where he hiked. His wilderness hikes were into the wild areas of Maine where he sought to find the primeval America. He developed a greater understanding of civilization after his journeys into wilderness area and believed in a balance of both. Henry was influenced by Indian spiritual thought and referenced India's sacred texts in his writings. He followed various Hindu customs such as eating rice, playing the flute and doing yoga.

Going into the wilds was seen by some as an unhealthy way of life for Thoreau.

His response was,

"We are receiving our portion of the infinite. The art of life? ...I do not remember any page which will tell me how to spend this afternoon. I do not so much wish to know how to economize time as how to spend it... The scenery, when it is truly seen, reacts on the life of the seer. How to live. How to get the most life... How to extract its honey from the flower of the world. That is my every-day business. I am as busy as a bee about it. I ramble all over the fields on that errand, and am never so happy as when I feel myself heavy with honey and wax."

Thoreau spoke out adamantly against the "blind and unmanly love of wealth." He was greatly concerned that humans were losing their connection to the land. Thoreau was clear that humanity was using its energy on all things "business" and the love of money. He said that humans should study nature because an estrangement from the land would "wither" a person's senses. To Thoreau "The mass of men lead lives of quiet desperation."

Leaving some areas untouched for animals to have a safe refuge was Thoreau's consistent theme. More than a decade before Congress made Yellowstone a National Park Thoreau publicly stated that there should be national preserves for animals to exist so that humans might seek inspiration and recreation. Thoreau protested destruction of landscapes and wildlife in his journal, but he really didn't promote public action. He was a philosopher who began the thought process about conserving the land. His writings had a great influence on the development of the National Park System in later years.

"I should not obtrude my affairs so much on the notice of my readers if very particular inquiries had not been made by my townsmen concerning my mode of life, which some would call impertinent, though they do not appear to me at all impertinent, but, considering the circumstances, very natural and pertinent. Some has asked what I got to eat; if I did not feel lonesome; if I was not afraid, and the like. Others have been curious to learn what portion of my income I devoted to charitable purposes; and some who have large families, how many poor children I maintained. Unfortunately, I am confined to this theme by the narrowness of my experience. Moreover, I, on my side, require of every writer, first or last, a simple and sincere account of his own life, and not merely what he has heard of other men's lives. I trust that none will stretch the seams in putting on the coat, for it may do good service to him who it fits"

Henry David Thoreau may not have been the first person to promote hunting animals without a gun, but he did stand with the protection of nature. He said the wonder of this kind of hunting brought pleasure and was a peaceful and gentle alternative to the normal way of destroying life rather than living with nature.

Long after Thoreau's death his philosophical observations about ecological patterns, forest growth, fire destruction of forests, human damage on the natural areas, and how everything was regenerated by the animal patterns and how wind dispersed the life bringing seeds for new growth his writings continue to gift environmentalists. Because of Thoreau's very detailed writings researchers have received an abundance of data used by ecologists in the study of global warming and environmental signs of our earth's demise.

Henry David Thoreau died May 6, 1862 after many years of battling tuberculosis. He lived with nature and a healthy life of exercise and a good diet and was certainly not a person who would be expected to die very young. During year two of the Civil War Henry wrote his last letter to his sister. He said, "I am enjoying existence as much as ever, and regret nothing."

JOHN WESLEY POWELL, 1834-1902

The Explorer's Words of Warning

"It is thus that, under conditions of civilization, the great forests of the arid land are being swept from the mountains and plateaus. Before the white man came the natives systematically burned over the forest lands with each recurrent year as one of the great hunting economies. By this process little destruction of timber was accomplished; but protected by civilized men, forests are rapidly disappearing. The needles, cones, and brush, together with the leaves of grass and shrubs below, accumulate when not burned annually and thus a spark sets off a blazing inferno." John Wesley Powell

John Wesley Powell was born to Joseph Powell and Mary Dean Powell, emigrants from England, on March 24, 1834, in Mount Morris, New York. Joseph Powell, a self-made minister, raised his family with Bible reading and much physical labor. Joseph Powell deliberately chose the name John Wesley for his second son in hopes that the appellation would inspire him to become a man of the cloth. This paternal desire only delayed Powell's scientific training and caused endless conflicts between him and his father. Although Powell did refuse to join the ministry, he did subscribe to many of his father's liberal beliefs. Perhaps the most important was the reverend's opposition to slavery.

John Wesley Powell's education came under the jurisdiction of George Crookham at age nine because the public-school children in Jackson, Ohio, continually physically abused Powell because of his superior intelligence and his vocal support against the evils of slavery. The jealous nature of his classmates in no way slowed down Powell's craving for knowledge. It was actually a great turning point in Powell's life because it was in Crookham's museum and study that John Wesley Powell's real education began.

While studying under Crookham, Powell's enthusiasm for natural history and scientific studies took on a new level which was to increase continually for the remainder of his life. Powell's education included botany, geology, philosophy, archeology, ethnology, chemistry, history, and literature. Field trips were taken frequently and research in every area of science was undertaken.

From the time of his boyhood, when he had labored from dawn to dusk on a frontier farm, Powell's intellect, ambitions, and dreams transcended the ordinary and restricted courses open to most persons born to his social level and the privations and backwoods environment he knew. He craved knowledge and as a youth was attracted by natural phenomena. A freshwater clam, a woodland plant, a ledge of rock, the contours of hills against the sky, fascinated him and he knew no peace until he had identified them, discovered the forces that had created and shaped them, and awarded them their proper place in the evolution of the earth. Early experiences and the education he acquired had stirred in him a devotion to science that was indestructible and had set him upon a road that he understood, but had no ending, for always there would be new mysteries to be solved.

After moving to Wisconsin, Powell continued his education through grammar school and college. He also taught at the elementary and secondary level for a time. At the conclusion of each year of teaching, Powell spent the summer months studying the environment of areas in Wisconsin, Ohio, and many parts of the Mississippi River. Most of Powell's work was around streams and rivers because he found it the best place to study the history of the earth. As the years passed, Powell toured many Midwestern streams making an extensive collection of mollusks and plants. Each of his trips brought him new excitement and a deeper understanding of nature.

As one of the founders of the Illinois State Historical Society, Powell suggested in 1861 that the Society hire a general commissioner and curator, who could give full time to the Society and whose duty it would be to superintend the research and collections, take charge of the museum, carry on the exchanges, and make the distributions. Powell, of course, was appointed to the position. Powell's own collections were the beginning of the museum and by this time he had amassed an impressive collection of plants, animals, fossils and mollusks. His reputation as a naturalist was firmly established.

That same year Powell's life took another direction. On May 3, 1861, President Abraham Lincoln called for 42,000 volunteers to save the Union. John Wesley Powell, a slender bearded man of twenty-seven, responded by enlisting in the army. During the war, two significant events occurred in his life. In November, 1861, General Ulysses S. Grant gave him a week's furlough to marry his first cousin and childhood sweetheart, Emma Dean. Six months later Powell's right arm was shattered by a minie ball in the battle of Shiloh. Doctors amputated the infected arm. Within two months Powell returned to active duty and participated in the battles of Vicksburg and Nashville. Throughout these engagements, his interest in science continued. Fossil seashells uncovered in trenches were sent home for his collection.

When the war ended, Major Powell became a professor of geology at Illinois Wesleyan University. While there, and later at Illinois Normal University, he frequently took his classes on walking trips to deal with the natural sciences firsthand. Additionally, he turned into a persuasive lecturer and organizer, and succeeded in having the Illinois State Legislature appropriate $2,500 for the Illinois Natural History Museum. When he was named curator of that museum, he wanted to provide the museum with comprehensive and valuable displays that would open new and greater opportunities to college students. Powell's suggestion was that specimens should be obtained from other regions. The Colorado Rockies was a good place to start. A new chapter in his life had begun.

If any man was prepared to deal with the wild American West, it was John Wesley Powell. He had labored on a farm, struggled for an education, navigated the Mississippi River alone, trekked across Wisconsin and Illinois on foot, and successfully commanded a battery of soldiers in two of the hardest fought battles of the Civil War. He was a leader, and he was fearless.

On his first trip to the Rockies, Major Powell and his wife were accompanied by twelve men with scientific backgrounds. The expedition had two missions: to broaden the collections of the natural history museum and to climb Pikes Peak. The expedition was very successful and proved to be the first of many Powell expeditions which would lead to a study of the west that none before or after would match.

Even before Powell had returned from his first expedition he was making plans for another to take place the following year. Powell's second expedition to the Rockies was to study the surrounding country of great canyons and valleys and immense mesas. This topographical and geological knowledge would give him a better understanding of the problems to be faced the next summer in the exploration of the Colorado River for which he was making plans even before the second expedition. The second expedition was funded by Powell's own university salary and donations from a few educational institutions. The railroad provided free travel. The Smithsonian Institution loaned scientific instruments. The federal government furnished rations.

During the second Powell expedition, the group scaled Long's Peak, which had never been previously climbed. Powell also made contact with the chief of the Ute Indians resulting in a life-long interest in ethnology. He studied the high altitude and mountain structure and observed the Gore Mountains, a wonderfully picturesque range which, up to this time, had been unexplored. Later the people of Colorado named the highest peak of the Gore Range

"Mount Powell." As in the first expedition many specimens were taken back to the Illinois Museum of Natural History for research purposes and for visitors to view.

Powell's studies were by no means a "stroll in the woods." Often times his studies were slowed down by the flooding of the rivers and streams which the expedition members lived by and crossed many times. Valuable equipment and supplies were lost to the floods. These harsh lessons and the unpredictability of the region's rivers were never forgotten by Major Powell.

When Powell suggested to Washington that he would like to survey the Colorado River most people thought the idea was ridiculous. Not many were willing to spend much time listening to a college professor who wanted to float off, probably to his death, on some western river. As a result, Powell's first expedition of the Colorado River gained little support from Washington. Powell's own salary from the Illinois Museum of Natural History and a few other donations from Illinois colleges were all the financial support he could compile. The truth was that if the railroads and express companies had not agreed to issue the requested passes and to transport his equipment and supplies free of charge, the Powell expedition to explore the Colorado River would have died in its infancy.

The Colorado River Expedition was far more than an adventure down the wildest river on the continent. It was a mission of science, and his search for specimens, geologic inspections, map work, and scientific observations were carried out in the face of enormous physical hazards.

Powell's scientific training was an important factor in the trip's success. He had done his homework on the canyon country and correctly predicted on the basis of available data that the journey could be made in boats, provided they were designed to withstand rough water. Powell's statement before the river expedition proved to be even more true than he had figured.

Powell's words began his account of his descent of the unknown Colorado River, one of the most daring feats of exploration in the natural history of the West.

"It is believed that the Grand Canyon of the Colorado will give the best geological section on the continent. Here are seen the central forces that formed the continent; here more striking studies in physical geography, geology, and natural history, than are proffered

anywhere else. May 24, 1869, the good people of Green River City turn out to see us start. We raise our little flag, push the boats from shore, and the swift current carries us down."

The exploration of the Colorado River was indeed a daring feat and the price for recording the natural history was high. Powell and his men, on several occasions, encountered disasters. Their first point on the Green River where one boat was lost and several pieces of scientific instruments were lost was appropriately named Disaster Falls.

After several grueling days of rapid after rapid, Powell recorded one scene of beauty by which he was deeply moved. "A dozen gleaming cascades are seen," exclaimed Powell.

> *"Pines and firs stand on the rocks, and aspens overhang the brooks. The rocks below are red and brown, set in deep shadows, but above they are buff and vermillion, and stand in the sunshine. It seems a long way up to the world of sunshine and open sky, and a long way down to the end of this canyon. Never before have I received such an, impression of the vast heights of these canyon walls."*

Powell's 1869 achievement of conquering the Colorado River made him a national hero. Invitations to speak poured upon him from every type of organization, from religious, historical, fraternal, and professional societies. Powell had learned things from this trip that would once again change the direction of his life.

In the spring of 1870, at the age of thirty-six, Major Powell began a fight he would continue for the remainder of his active life. He sought to give knowledge to the American people, and he struggled unceasingly to prevent despoliation of western resources not already destroyed or irrecoverably lost to unscrupulous interests.

Two years after his Colorado River Expedition Powell persuaded Congress to give him $10,000 to organize a second Colorado River expedition which became known as the "Geographical and Topographical Survey of the Colorado River of the West." It was not only better equipped than the first but included four trained scientists as well as an artist and a professional photographer.

During the second Colorado River expedition, Powell accumulated a storehouse of land wisdom about the West. This expedition did not just explore the river but studied the problems of the surrounding land and its people. He studied the climate and resources of the forests, plateaus, and streams. His understanding of the land, its water and watersheds and the role of man as a geological factor in a fragile landscape made him an intellectual giant during his time.

For almost ten years after his river expedition, Powell studied the ecology of the plains and high plateaus. The cycles of rivers and rainfall, the village life and conservation practices of the Utah Mormons, and the land-use ideas of the Indians and Spanish-American settlers enabled him to grasp the essentials of order of the West. In his 1878 pamphlet entitled "Report on the Lands of the Arid Region of the United States" he suggested two legislative measures that advocated drastic revisions in federal statutes governing the settlement and development of the western public domain. The bills proffered radical departures from existing practices that would have given the federal government full control of new western water and grazing projects. Powell pointed out that the rainfall in most of the West was not enough to sustain an economy based on traditional patterns of agriculture; and that many of the homesteaders moving to these arid lands were doomed to fail. Powell's words were not heeded seriously until the 1930's.

As Powell became even more involved in his scientific work he also had many honors bestowed on him. He was president of the American Association for the Advancement of Science. He was a member of the exclusive National Academy of Sciences and had won the Cuvier Prize of the French Academy of Sciences. He received honorary degrees from Columbia, Harvard, Illinois, and Heidelberg Universities. Besides his many honors he founded the Bureau of American Ethnology at the Smithsonian Institute and helped establish the United States Geological Survey of which he became director in 1881.

Powell's bureaus flourished under his direction. To his way of thinking, geology was not simply what the dictionary said it was: scientific study of solid matter for the purpose of learning the history of the earth and its life. Powell wanted the Geologic Survey to concern itself with the earth's history, with rocks, minerals, and fossils. Powell's number of interests never ceased to increase. New investigation was pursued by Powell on a continuous basis. As if geology and ethnology were not enough, he also had his men involved in hydrology, soil classification, topographical mapping, paleontology, physiography, irrigation and of course the land reform laws.

Even though Powell worked continually at an exhausting pace, he still took the time to make lecture tours throughout the United States thrilling audiences with stereopticon views of Native Americans, the Hopi towns, and the spectacular scenery of the canyons of the Colorado.

From the very early years of his life, John Wesley Powell was developing himself as a naturalist. Powell was schooled as a naturalist, intimate with the earth, its structure, and ever-changing face. He was equally familiar with Native peoples and scholars and the endless variety of plants and animals. Powell thought in terms of nature. He was a scientist seized with the optimism of discovery and with faith in the ultimate attainment of absolute truth by the methods of science. Everything Powell worked to accomplish has impacted environmental health into the present.

Powell, in the 1880's, was one of the first people to speak out about land and water use in America. Powell's view on controlled burning of forest land to save forests was not understood during his lifetime and is not understood in many circles today.

Powell sums up his feelings on controlled burning.

"I have witnessed more than a dozen fires in Colorado. Compared with the trees destroyed by fire, those used by man sink into insignificance. Some years ago I mapped the forests of Utah, and found that about half had been thus consumed since the occupation of the country by civilized man. So the fires rage throughout the Rocky Mountains and through the Sierras and the Cascades. They are so frequent and of such vast proportions that the surveyors of the land often find their work impeded or wholly obstructed by clouds of smoke. There is a practical method by which forests can be preserved. If herds and flocks crop the grasses and trample the leaves and cones into the ground, they make trails through the woods and destroy the conditions most favorable to the spread of fire. Living forests are a delight, for in beauty and grandeur they are unexcelled; but dead forests present scenes of desolation that fill the soul with sadness."

Throughout his life Powell developed a comprehensive knowledge of western resources, and in a time when resources meant gold, silver, coal, or iron, to most men, he had the vision to add timber, soil, water, and dam sites. Powell's beliefs about these new resources were listened to by very few individuals. To conserve these resources from the wastage, folly, and graft that were already threatening them, he conceived what he called the "general plan" of governmental control, a plan that involved whole new concepts of law; new patterns of economic and political and social organization; new designs for agriculture; and whole philosophies of cooperation and governmental assistance.

What Powell proposed was rendered absolutely essential by the nature of western terrain and western climate. But what he proposed was totally at odds with the myths and shibboleths of the main western settlement; the fantasies of the common man and the 160 acre farm; and the yeoman freehold that had supposedly bred and perpetuated the self-reliance of better-watered frontiers.

In Powell's "Report on the Lands of the Arid Region of the United States" he suggested legislative measures that advocated drastic revisions in Federal statutes governing the settlement and development of the Western public domain. It was a document vital to the survival of the Western United States not taken seriously until almost twenty years after its publication. Had the report been heeded; waste and exploitation would have been stopped and development of a region that included 40 percent of the United States could have been saved. But, the forces of ignorance, the Chamber of Commerce ballyhoo, corrupt bureaucrats, unconscionable bankers, industrialists, and the deceitful propaganda dinned into the public's ears by railroaders, land swindlers, and racketeers of every conceivable type, were arrayed against him in formidable force. The West was raped and all Powell could do was watch. A hard lesson for America to learn, but in many areas we have learned through Powell's contributions.

Powell's own words explain his strong commitment to saving the environment.

"The solution to the problem of having enough water for the arid lands is no simple one. In brief, the waters must be divided among the states, but there is no law for it, and the states are in conflict. In the end everyone loses because the land and its inhabitants disappear while the conflict continues.

"The great forests that clothe the hills, plateaus, and mountains with verdure must be saved from devastation by fire and preserved for the use of man, that the sources of water may be protected, that farms may be fenced and homes built and that all this wealth of forest may be distributed among the people. The grasses that are to feed the flocks and herds must be protected and utilized. The great mineral deposits—the fuel of the future, the iron for the railroads, and the gold and silver for our money—must be kept ready to the hand of industry and the brain of enterprise."

Powell suggested that all streams and creeks in a group of mountains combine and form a drainage system of a hydrographic basin, a unit of country well defined in nature, for it is bounded above and on each side by heights of land that rise as crests to split water coming down. Thus, one hydraulic basin is segregated from another hydraulic basin by nature. In such a basin of the arid region the irrigable lands lie below, not on the riverside, but on the mesas and low plains. Above this land the water supply is found. Powell suggested that the people who farm below should manage the water supply from above. The problem was that someone else controlled those water supplies.

Those people who farmed were interested in the forests that crowned the heights of the hydrographic basin. Powell could see that if they were to permit the forests to be destroyed, the source of their water supply would be injured and the timber values wiped out. Powell wanted the people directly interested to perform the task of guarding the forests. He also said that a forestry organization under the hands of the general government would become a hot-bed of corruption.

Powell believed that people in a district would have common interests, common duties, and would work together for common purposes. He wanted those people to organize, under national and state laws, an irrigation district and hydrographic basin and to make their own laws for the division of the waters; for the protection and use of the forests; for the protection of the pasturage on the hills; and for the use of the political powers.

John Wesley Powell's life's work centered around saving the natural resources. He believed that without a different system of land and water management the entire environment of the West virtually would be destroyed. His words were not heeded until it was almost too late. He knew, as if being a prophet, that the land system of the country in the West was not suitable for the area of the arid region. He foresaw dust bowls, watershed destruction, animal depletion and the general erosion of the land in the West because of improper management of land and water.

When Powell explored the Colorado River, he had looked back through sixty million years. He believed that the river had not cut its way down through mountains for thousands of feet, but had cut its channel as the folds were lifted. The Colorado River had been running before the rock formations had been folded to form mountain ranges and he proved it through exploration. His theory had not been accepted until after he made his voyage.

John Wesley Powell, as Audubon and Thoreau before him, stands out as a giant among men, then and now. His contributions are many and it seems almost impossible for one man to have given so much to the preservation of our country.

Major Powell changed the geologic views of his elders through his exploration of the Colorado River. He proved that the mountains were not raised as peaks but that great blocks of the earth's crust rose slowly and from this the mountains were carved by storms. Mountains did not form clouds. Clouds formed mountains. By lifting the mountains into the clouds this permits storms to gather about them carving out canyons and valleys, leaving plateaus and mountains embossed on the surface and beats the rocks into sands and carries them to the plains and out into the sea. The canyons presented the greatest geological discovery on the continent. Powell compounded and advanced a new concept, the concept of the cycle of topographic development. He laid the foundation of a new science: physiography.

To the paleontologists, Powell gave unknown types of fossils. To the ethnologists, he gave Indian vocabularies, artifacts, and the sites of ancient villages. To the zoologists, he also gave new species of animals and new samples of plants to the botanists.

Powell made the last important exploration within the continental United States. Before his time, the map from Washington had a great unmapped space of 300 to 500 miles long and 100 to 200 miles broad. Through his work with the United States Geologic Survey, which he helped begin and also headed, a topographic and geologic map of most every area of the United States came into being. Through his explorations Powell discovered the last discovered river in America, the Escalante, and the last discovered mountains, the Henry's, in the United States.

Throughout all his work, his greatest gift was in the area of land and water resource management. Ignorance of the true natural conditions in the west was appalling during Powell's life-time. Powell developed a comprehensive knowledge of western resources. Not the resources of gold, silver, coal, and iron which most men knew of, but timber, soil, water, and dam sites, the irreplaceable resources upon which a continuing society in the West would have to be built.

Had he been listened to in time, Powell might have spared us many things: the dust bowls of the 1930's, the rivers, the erosion and loss of soil, the ruination of watersheds, the floods that in the lower reaches of the great rivers bore testimony to the malpractices at the headwaters. At the end of the 1880's he almost had it in his grasp, until the politician and the western land, cattle, and water interests broke him.

The ideas and proposals advanced in Powell's work were used as building blocks and were incorporated into the Newlands Reclamation Act of 1902, the legislation of 1933 establishing the Tennessee Valley Authority, the Taylor Grazing Act of 1934, and the laws creating national forests and interstate water compacts. They came late, but not altogether too late.

Almost every individual who is involved in the conservation of western soil, water, and watersheds, or dam sites uses Powell's "Report of the Arid Lands" like a bible. Every student of geology knows him, for he and his collaborators wrote one of the early and indispensable chapters in that science. Finally, members of the fraternity of river tourists, the white-water enthusiasts who do for sport what Powell did cautiously and at great peril, know him, and some know his book *The Exploration of the Colorado River* almost by heart. Powell was a true naturalist whose type of contributions have not and perhaps will not be matched.

Powell recognized the West's water limitations and argued for limited development and conservation practices. However, after many years of pushing the Land Reform Act and the Water Rights Bills, Powell resigned from the Geologic Survey. It was in 1902 that President Theodore Roosevelt signed the bill that created the Bureau of Reclamation which started the wheels rolling on the very land and water reform bills which Powell had suggested so many years before. Major John Wesley Powell suffered a heart attack that same year and died shortly thereafter. Most of his dreams, which finally were becoming reality, were never witnessed by him.

JOHN MUIR, 1838-1914

The Voice of the Conservation Movement

"God has cared for these trees, saved them from drought, disease, avalanches, and a thousand tempests and floods. But he cannot save them from fools." John Muir

John Muir, the third child and eldest boy of eight children, was born the twenty-first of April, 1838, to Daniel and Ann Gilrye Muir in Dunbar, Scotland. The first eleven years of John Muir's life were spent in Scotland living like most children in Dunbar. School began at age three for Muir in a very strict academic setting coupled with a heavy religious upbringing. In school, Muir had natural wild tendencies very similar to other children, but he always had a deep desire for learning. His readings contained natural history sketches that excited him very much and left a deep impression which stayed with him for life. Some reading lessons described American forests and Muir dreamed of wandering through the forests looking at every minute detail. One of John Muir's favorite stories was about the passenger pigeons described by the famous naturalist, John James Audubon. Muir studied Audubon's travels with great anticipation not knowing the influence Audubon's writing would have on his life.

Muir's earliest recollections of the country were gained on short walks with his grandfather. While out in the wilds around his native town, he seemed to drink into his being everything that was wild. Along the rugged seashore he explored the pools among the rocks where shells, seaweeds, eels, and crabs excited his childish wonder and when the tide was low, he found adventurous recreation by climbing the craggy headlands. Young Muir loved to wander in the fields to hear birds sing and interpret what the smallest of the plants revealed. From early in life Muir was always fond of everything that was wild and as he grew older, he seemed to grow fonder and fonder of wild places and wild creatures.

Daniel Muir, John's father, ruled his family with an iron fist and the Bible. Unaccepted actions by the Muir children were severely punished by whippings and a mandatory memorization of the scriptures. John Muir had his share of the punishment and probably more because of a tendency toward wildness about him.

At the age of eleven the Muir family moved to the United States and to the state of Wisconsin and thus began John Muir's baptism into nature's wonderland. In his book *The Story of My Boyhood and Youth*, Muir describes his first moments at their Wisconsin farm.

> *"Just as we arrived at the shanty, before we had time to look at it or the scenery about it, brother David and I jumped down in a hurry off the load of household goods, for we had discovered a blue jay's nest, and in a minute or two we were up in the tree beside it, feasting our eyes on the beautiful green eggs and beautiful birds—our first memorable discovery."*

From this moment on Muir discovered new wonders every day. But those first days and weeks of enjoyment and freedom of the wildness were also mingled with the hard work of making a farm. Hard work and daily worship made up much of John Muir's life the first few years after moving to America.

Muir was ploughing the family farm at the age of twelve and days began at four in the morning and ended around nine in the evening. Work continued even if illness struck because the Scotch people believed work done even when sick was good punishment for every fault, imagined or committed. Through it all Muir continued to have that special yearning for knowledge. He learned about the outdoors through direct association with the environment. In non-working hours, he studied the plants and animals or read literature related to the environment. He read after everyone went to bed at night because he felt a few minutes of intellectual discovery were golden blocks of knowledge which could never be taken away.

John Muir's life with his folks almost seemed to be an introduction or initiation into his later life as a naturalist. After eight years of working at building a farm for his father, and just when it seemed perfect order had been victoriously accomplished, Muir's father purchased another area of wild land and the difficult work began all over again. While swimming in the farm pond on one occasion, Muir almost drowned, and on another occasion while digging a well for the farm he almost succumbed to carbonic acid gas poisoning. Harsh as it was, Muir could not have accomplished the things he did in later life without the upbringing his father gave him. He learned from his father the capacity for enjoyment and a great love of nature. His father's love of plants and flowers was transmitted to him enabling him to take life and death in stride as if he understood philosophically how it all fit together in the universe.

As John Muir grew into a young man, he applied his knowledge of mathematics and science to the art of inventing. He invented a self-setting sawmill, waterwheels, door locks, thermometers, hygrometers, pyrometers, clocks, barometers, lamp lighters and many other gadgets. On occasion he even used this art to obtain pocket money for another excursion into the wilderness.

Muir's first real excursion into the wilderness was hiking the Wisconsin River studying botany and geology. Perhaps the main lesson of this trip was the great destructive power of the lumber industry. This first long exposure to the wilderness made a tremendous impression on him. It gave him a way to measure civilization which he found generally lacking. To go into the wilderness to find the plan that governs the relations existing between human beings and nature seemed the most worthwhile thing he could do.

From the time of John Muir's earliest childhood wanderings, he was continually looking forward to the time when all wild fellow creatures would be granted their sacredness with all living things. He lived his life ever striving to give those things considered other life forms by Homo sapiens a fitting home just as he had.

While Muir was growing up, it was considered a great sport for boys to join together to hunt birds, squirrels, and every other unclaimed, unprotected live thing of any size. It was to Muir a shameful sport which he never wanted anything to do with. He was also proud of the fact that during his childhood years his family killed only one deer. Muir, a preservationist, claimed that deer like other animals had just as much right to be on this earth as any human. In later years in the sawmills, he was also happy to say he had only cut downed timber so as not to disturb the growing forests. Forests, he claimed, would thin out themselves just as they had for millennium before.

After being accepted at the University of Wisconsin, Muir studied botany to fill in the gaps which his intellectual being needed. During class and at every open opportunity he wandered about on long excursions gathering specimens and keeping them fresh in a bucket in order to study them in more detail at night. During vacations from school, Muir studied botany around the Great Lakes in Ontario, and through parts of Wisconsin, Indiana, and Illinois.

It was at the university that he first studied the subject of glaciers through the writings of Louis Agassiz of Switzerland who is considered the father of glaciology. His study of Agassiz' methods for measuring the movement of glaciers was the basis for his investigation of the glacial origins of Yosemite about which he wrote in later years.

While Muir was at the University of Wisconsin his social life also broadened. His friendship with Jeanne and Ezra Carr proved invaluable throughout the remainder of his life. Dr. Ezra Carr, his chemistry and geology professor, opened to him the very latest scientific studies. Mrs. Carr, herself a talented botanist, artist, and musician, taught him humanities.

During one period of time off from school, while working in a sawmill, he suffered a severe eye injury which confined him to a dark room for many long days. It was during this confinement that he concluded that life was too brief and uncertain, and time too precious, to waste on trivial matters. Muir's perceptions of the world came to fruition as he aged and he determined that if his eyesight was spared he would devote the remainder of his life to a study of natural history. It was at this time that he decided to give up mechanical inventions and the university life and devote his time to the study of the inventions of God.

Muir's more intimate friends observed in him a strange kind of restlessness, an inward desire to forsake all and begin life in the wilderness. When asked where he was going, Muir replied,

"I wish I knew where I was going. Doomed to be carried of the spirit into the wilderness I suppose. I wish I could be more moderate in my desires, but I cannot, and so there is no rest. I am leaving the University of Wisconsin for the University of the Wilderness and my address is John Muir-Earth-Planet-Universe."

After leaving Wisconsin, Muir began his famous thousand mile walk to the Gulf of Mexico which later became the subject of one of his published books. He traveled through the Kentucky forests and caves and into the Cumberland Mountains, the first real mountains he climbed. From Kentucky he traveled through Georgia, Florida, and Cuba studying all kinds of plants with a power of exact observation that was at the same time scientific and aesthetic.

Muir's love of nature was so largely a part of his religion that he naturally chose Biblical language when he sought to express his feelings. No Old Testament Prophet could have taken his call more seriously, or have entered upon his mission more fervently. During his walk to the Gulf Muir wrote a prose as strong as any in the English language. His writings had a magical effect on the reader who shared his works.

After his travels to the Gulf, Muir headed for California and the High Sierra which became his home for the next ten years. While out on his first excursion in Yosemite, he wrote to his sister Sarah,

"I have nearly all of every day to myself to climb, sketch, write, meditate, and botanize. My foot has pressed no floor but that of the mountains for many a day. I am far from the ways and pursuits of man. I am with Nature in the grandest, most divine of all her earthly dwelling places."

Muir understood nature both as a mechanism and as a form of wisdom. In the wilderness, he was a combination of mountain sage and a desert father of old. His mind was searching for new knowledge and could focus in on the smallest flower or consider the world's natural history. When he discovered a new plant, he sat down beside it, to make its acquaintance and interpret what it had to teach. When he discovered a mountain or a rock he climbed about it, comparing it with others, making its relation to living or dead glaciers, streams of water, and avalanches of snow as he besought to account for its existence and character.

While living and working in Yosemite he became a well-known interpreter in the Valley. As he became known in the area he had the chance to meet a number of famous people. One of his most memorable experiences was the meeting of Ralph Waldo Emerson, who became a very close friend and a turning influence in Muir's life.

Muir's early studies of glaciers played a part in his stay at Yosemite because his theory of the formation of the Valley was in direct conflict with the geologists of the time. Muir sent his first thoughts on Yosemite Glaciers to the New York Tribune which became the first published statement of the ice erosion theory to account for the origin of Yosemite. Soon after this, Muir began to write for publication. He contributed a series of articles to the "Overland Monthly" and became a nationally known figure in the area of environmental interpretation and conservation.

John Muir knew the Sierra Nevada and the Yosemite Valley's watershed better than anyone, and because he saw it all as an invention of God he wanted to determine the mechanics of the Sierra's formation. But, he could not have accomplished what he did in the Sierra Nevada without his extremely simple backcountry outlook. From the beginning of his wanderings, he saw traveling with the bare necessities as the primary virtue of a mobile wilderness style. Mostly, he ate plain bread but on occasion he would take dried meat and fruit. His food style was based on the knowledge that he could go without food for up to eight or ten days provided he had water. Experienced in fasting, he would expend himself to the limit, physically and mentally, on his trips and then come down and eat, rest, and recover. While he made his home in the Sierra Nevada, he also journeyed to and explored the wilderness areas of Nevada and Utah.

A decade after first setting foot in the Sierra Nevada, he decided his work was virtually completed there and he left for the first of five trips to Alaska. Alaska made an overwhelming impression on him, for here were the kinds of glaciers whose effects he had studied in the Sierra Nevada. While in Alaska, he became the first person of the West to see Glacier Bay. Sometime later, on his third trip to Alaska, he visited one of the largest glaciers which is now named Muir Glacier.

At the age of forty-six, Muir married Louise Strentzel, whose family had a large fruit ranch near San Francisco. He took over the management of the ranch and for the next ten years expanded and developed the area. During this time, he still continued his travels throughout western America.

With the founding of the Sierra Club in 1892, Muir stepped fully into the politics of conservation. By the 1890's it was clear that the negative exploitation of the wilderness by corporate monopolies, carried on with increasing vigor since the Civil War, had to stop. Muir was the master publicist of the conservation movement and a lobbyist for conservation at the highest levels of government. His articles and public proposals and his book *Mountains of California* were instrumental in creating the sentiment for preservation and conservation in America. At the turn of the century, John Muir had become the Senator-At-Large for America's natural environment.

Muir felt the same reverence for the land, the sense of wholeness and oneness, that had been experienced by the Indians and the early naturalists. His journeys enabled him to know this continent as few others knew it before or have known it since. These were not just walks but revelations, a nature lover's Pilgrim's Progress. On his walk to the Gulf he wrote the following thoughts:

"*A numerous class of men are painfully astonished whenever they find anything, living or dead, in all God's universe, which they cannot eat or render in some way useful to themselves. Why should man value himself as more than a small part of the one great unit of creation? The universe would be incomplete without man; but it would also be incomplete without the smallest transmicroscopic creature that dwells beyond our conceitful eye and knowledge. From the dust of the earth the Creator has made Homo sapiens from the same material he has made every other creature. They are earthborn companions and our fellow mortals. Plants are credited with but dim and uncertain sensation and minerals with positively none at all. But why may not even a mineral arrangement of matter be endowed with sensation of a kind that we in our blind exclusive perfection can have no manner of communication with?"*

Muir's early travels in the Midwest made him heartsick as he saw the wanton destruction of timber and wildlife. After reaching Yosemite, he found evidence of the destructive results of overgrazing from sheep and cattle.

Early in his career Muir came to a conclusion that decisively affected his own future and to some degree the future of the country. Wilderness freedom, like political freedom, was perennially in danger and could be maintained only by eternal vigilance. He became convinced it was necessary to preserve large tracts of choice lands in permanent public ownership. His overall conviction was that the best parts of the woodlands and the wilderness should be preserved in perpetuity as sanctuaries of the human spirit.

By the end of the century it was clear that negative exploitation of wilderness by corporate monopolies had to end. Land, mining, and timber speculators, together with cattle and sheep interests, were running rampant over the wilderness. After witnessing lumbermen cutting magnificent trees thousands of years old Muir wrote one of his first newspaper articles entitled "God's First Temples—How Shall We Preserve Our Forests?" This article was the first appeal for the protection of the forests.

John Muir's commitment to nature was clear. He lived his beliefs to the utmost degree. He believed the universe would be incomplete without humankind, but that it would also be incomplete without the smallest creatures that dwell on this planet. Humankind could protect itself, but it was absolutely necessary to preserve large tracts of land in public ownership as sanctuaries for living organisms and should be used for nothing more, thereby protecting other living creatures and their homes.

During the first year of his residence in the Yosemite Valley, Muir became convinced that the Valley had not been formed by a cataclysm, but by long, slow, natural processes in which ice played the major part. This idea, which was in direct conflict with the geologists of the time, was proven correct and has helped people become more aware of the formation of the environment around them.

When Muir discovered a new plant he sat down beside it for a time to make its acquaintance and to learn about its characteristics. When he discovered a mountain or rock he climbed about it, comparing it with its neighbors, determining its relation to living or dead glaciers, streams of water, and avalanches of snow in seeking to account for its existence and character. Muir's writings on his discoveries are indeed a great contribution to society because through reading his works a person can feel and understand each plant, animal, tree, and mountain which he comes in contact with and can become more aware of the necessity for the preservation of our country's environment. Also, the capacity for enjoyment of nature will possibly be enhanced to the point of becoming intimate with each part of nature no matter how small or how large.

Muir was the master publicist of the preservation movement and a lobbyist for preservation at the highest levels of government. Muir's work greatly influenced Presidents Harrison, Cleveland, and Roosevelt to establish close to 200,000,000 acres of forest reserves as public lands. He had a hand in the creation of the United States Forest Service and also helped establish many national parks and monuments. Muir played a vital role in establishing eight of our superb national parks, which includes Sequoia, Yosemite, Mount Rainier, Crater Lake, Glacier, Mesa Verde, Grand Canyon and Olympic. He also helped establish a dozen national monuments. It was to a large degree because of his leadership that the national park idea became part of the preservation movement.

Because of his success in the preservation movement, Muir formed a private organization of mountaineers and conservationists to carry on his fight for the wilderness. Out of this effort came the Sierra Club, a crusading organization to explore, enjoy and protect the nation's scenic resources. The Sierra Club today is a prime mover in increasing America's environmental awareness.

Perhaps John Muir's greatest gift to America is his restatement of the American Indian idea of wilderness as a place to go in search of a vision. To Muir, the true wilderness experience was far more than mere exposure to nature. He saw that it began with heightened sensibilities and ended in exactness of observation. He also saw that men were eyewitnesses to creation if only they opened their eyes to it.

More and more Americans see, as Muir did, that in this increasingly commercial civilization there must be natural sanctuaries where commercialism is non-existent, where power plants, dams, billboards and subdivisions are permanently prohibited, where every man may enjoy the spiritual exhilaration of the wilderness. Each day more and more Americans see the significance of John Muir's words:

> "Walk away quietly in any direction and taste the freedom of the mountaineer. Camp out among the grasses and gentians of glacial meadows, in craggy garden nooks full of nature's darlings. Climb the mountains and get their good tidings, Nature's peace will flow into you as sunshine flows into trees. The winds will blow their own freshness into you and the storms their energy, while cares will drop off like autumn leaves. As age comes on, one source of enjoyment after another is closed, but nature's sources never fail."

In his later years when his health began to fail Muir's travels increased and he saw more reckless exploitation of the land than ever. His travels took him to Europe visiting parks and forests where he sketched and studied botany along the way.

After his last adventure, during which he sketched and botanized the Amazon River, he returned to the final rounds of perhaps his greatest conservation fight: the battle to save Hetch Hetchy Valley in Yosemite National Park from being dammed and flooded by the city of San Francisco. The political issue was the inviolability of a national park, but the larger issue was saving the beautiful of the natural world. He lost the battle.

Shortly after the Hetch Hetchy battle Muir, trying desperately to finish his book *Travels to Alaska,* contracted pneumonia and died on Christmas Eve, 1914. Earth-Planet-Universe lost an intimate friend but his life had changed America in a unique way just as Audubon, Thoreau and Powell had before him.

Because of John Muir the thousands and thousands of people who go to the mountains, streams, and canyons of the West will choose to see them through his eyes. He has left our country with an awareness for the environment which will command the attention of people so long as human records endure.

> "If my soul could get away from this so-called prison, be granted all the list of attributes generally bestowed on spirits, my first ramble on spirit-wings would not be among the volcanoes of the moon. Nor should I follow the sunbeams to their sources in the sun. I should hover about the

beauty of our own good star. I should not go moping among the tombs, not around the artificial desolation of men. I should study Nature's laws in all their crossings and unions; I should follow magnetic streams to their source and follow the shores of our magnetic oceans. I should go among the rays of the aurora, and follow them to their beginnings, and study their dealings and communions with other powers and expressions of matter. And I should go to the very center of our globe and read the whole splendid page from the beginning. But my first journeys would be into the inner substance of flowers, and among the folds and mazes of Yosemite's falls. How grand to move about in the very tissue of falling columns, and in the very birthplace of their heavenly harmonies, looking outward as from windows of ever-varying transparency and staining!" John Muir

GIFFORD PINCHOT, 1865-1946

A Voice for Change in Forestry Practices

"Unless we practice conservation, those who come after us will have to pay the price of misery, degradation, and failure for the progress and prosperity of our day." Gifford Pinchot

Gifford Pinchot was born August 11, 1865, in Simsbury, Connecticut to James and Mary Jane Eno Pinchot. Both of Gifford's parents came from very wealthy and prominent families so he had an affluent style of living. At the same time, he had empathy for those of all levels of society.

James Pinchot, a businessman in New York City, was extremely interested in Europe's forestry system and was the author of various articles on the subject of forestry. James Pinchot was also the onetime vice-president of the American Forestry Association. Mary Jane Pinchot, a member of the Daughters of the American Revolution, directed her energies in that organization toward preventing waste of the nation's natural resources and at one point served as chairman of that organization's conservation committee.

Gifford Pinchot's father joined the first feeble voices for change in forestry practices and urged his son, who reveled in the outdoors, to consider forestry as a profession. At the time, however, there were no schools of forestry in the United States; the nation had no educationally prepared foresters and there were no jobs for foresters. Because of young Pinchot's fortune of being born into a wealthy family the first few years of his life were spent traveling in other countries. During the first nine years of his life he was accustomed to such close supervision by his father that his life was pampered and sheltered. But the strictness of his father in no way slowed down his inclination to demonstrate his rugged side.

Pinchot attended three private schools in New York City before he finished his scholastic career and entered his collegiate career at Yale University. Throughout his childhood and adolescent years he enjoyed the hobbies of fishing and insect study. His rugged life style and his yearning for adventure in the outdoors was always present throughout his schooling and continued with him to Yale, along with his father's desire for him to become a forester.

At Yale, Pinchot studied courses in science preparing for his future life as a forester. At that time the United States had no curriculums in forestry so after graduating from Yale he studied silviculture in France. He returned to the United States in 1890 to embark on a life-long career which no American had attempted before him.

Pinchot began his career as a forester as a consultant to Phelps, Dodge and Company in the management of their forest lands. After a tour of the forest land in America, Pinchot returned to the East to take charge of the Biltmore Forest of the Biltmore Estates owned by George Vanderbilt.

The Biltmore Forest became the beginning of practical forestry in America. It was the first piece of woodland in the United States to be put under a regular system of forest management with the objective to pay the owner while improving the forest. The Biltmore Forest was also the place where it was suggested that the Federal Government buy tracts of timberland and pursue the practice of forestry. Twenty years later this project was actually carried out. These early beginnings of practical forestry are of course credited to Gifford Pinchot.

After two years as Chief Forester to George Vanderbilt, Pinchot opened an office in New York City as a consulting forester and was soon employed by the state of New Jersey as a consultant to the Geological Survey. Pinchot's deep concern over the theft and destruction of the public timber and timberlands pushed him more and more into the public's eye as he spoke out and wrote on the terrible destruction of public lands. Pinchot had the clear eye of a scientist, a naturalist's love of the woods and open spaces, the moral fervor of an evangelist, and a politician's intuitions. His task, he was convinced, was to stop the practice of forest destruction in the United States, and to inaugurate the practice of forestry. During this period of his life he began his life time of work of saving the forests of the country.

"When I came home not a single acre of Government, state, or private timberland was under systematic forest management anywhere on the most richly timbered of all continents... When the Gay Nineties began, the common word for our forests was 'inexhaustible.' To waste timber was a virtue and not a crime. There would always be plenty of timber... The lumbermen regarded forest devastation as normal and second growth as a delusion of fools... And as for sustained yield, no such idea had ever entered their heads. The few friends the forest had were spoken of, when they were spoken of at all, as impractical theorists, fanatics, or

'denudatics,' more or less touched in the head. What talk there was about forest protection was no more to the average American than the buzzing of a mosquito, and just about as irritating."

As a result of his crusade he was appointed to the National Forest Commission to study the forest reserves in the West. To Pinchot's great delight, another crusader and somewhat of a hero to him was along to view the forests. The man was John Muir. A close friendship began which Pinchot and Muir enjoyed for a few years only to have it end in a bitter dispute over land use in Yosemite Valley. Working with the National Forest Commission and President Grover Cleveland, Pinchot helped more than double the Forest Reserves in the United States with one bill in Congress, the Forest Reserve Act of 1891.

Because of Pinchot's knowledge and training in forestry, the Commission appointed him Confidential Forest Agent. The job was to report on Forest Reserves, their condition and needs, and their relations to lumbering, agriculture, mining, grazing, commerce, and settlement. His assignment was to draw up a set of principles to govern future increase and decrease in the Reserves and apply them to individual cases. He was also to report a practical plan for the establishment of a Forest Service, with specific recommendations for individual reserves. Later that same year, 1898, Pinchot became Chief of the United States Forestry Division with the title of Chief Forester, the first in the history of the United States.

As Pinchot became more involved in forestry in America, he also became more involved in the political aspect of it. He lectured and wrote more on the forestry movement. He helped form the Society of American Foresters attempting to gain genuine respect for the profession of forestry. Along with his efforts to educate the public was his crusade to introduce forestry into the curriculum of schools and colleges. Foreseeing the need for professional education in forestry in the United States, he persuaded his father and mother to join with him in establishing a School of Forestry at his alma mater, Yale University, the first of its kind in America. He needed trained foresters for his organization and Yale would and did educate good men for him and the profession. A natural leader, he chose his men well, gave them authority, developed an esprit de corps and sent them forth to save the forests.

After many bitter political battles, of which Pinchot took a more than active part, the Forestry Bureau became the United States Forest Service and changed from the Department of Interior to the Department of Agriculture.

Pinchot and the Forest Service had to deal with the old and ingrained habit of exploitation of the West. The great special interests of the West, whose monopolies were threatened, threw lobbyists and press against the Forest Service such as Washington had never seen before. Because of its rapid growth and the zealousness of Pinchot, the Forest Service had more and more active enemies by far than any other government bureau. Pinchot seemed to thrive on the political battles and almost every waking hour saw him in some type of confrontation on Forest Service policies.

The big break for Pinchot, and for forestry, came when Theodore Roosevelt assumed the Presidency. The two men were already acquainted and for the next several years worked together for a common cause: to see if the forests could be saved and used simultaneously.

Grazers and loggers were assessed user fees, and for the first time grass and trees were managed in such a way that they could be replenished on a sustained-yield basis. Pinchot had the Forest Service dealing with trees, public lands, mining, agriculture, irrigation, stream flow, soil erosion, fish, game, and the animal industry. The multiple-use concept became the norm. Research became a high priority item in Pinchot's organization and he founded the Forestry Research Laboratory at Madison, Wisconsin. Pinchot made the Forest Service no organization of master and servant. It was a service of mutual effort for a common purpose. It was "come on, let's do it together," and not "you go and do it while I sit by and watch you." The chief driving force which made the Forest Service one of the best organizations under the government was not the desire to earn good money, but the urge to do good work in a good cause.

During the Roosevelt administration Pinchot began the conservation movement by formulating the Inland Waterways Commission to consider the relations of the streams to the use of all the great permanent natural resources and their conservation for the making and maintenance of prosperous homes. The Commission repeatedly warned against monopolistic control over forests, waters, lands and minerals. It emphasized the fact that an excessive share of the natural resources had been diverted to the enrichment of a few rather than preserved for the equitable benefit of the many. Pinchot also helped instigate the first Governor's Conference on Conservation which introduced to humankind the policy of conservation of natural resources.

Pinchot had begun a counter-movement to the destruction of the environment. He brought out the ideas which became Theodore Roosevelt's conservation program and sailing was smooth until the end of the Roosevelt administration. Roosevelt's follower, William Taft, did not feel the excitement of the cause as Pinchot did which produced several confrontations. The main confrontation being a fight with Taft's Secretary of the Interior, Richard Ballinger, implying Ballinger was corrupt in dealing with coal leases on Alaskan forest lands. Pinchot's reign as Chief Forester for the United States Forest Service came to an end.

After Pinchot's fiery exit from Taft's organization, he became involved in yet another pressure group to assist in the fight for conservation. From 1910 until the early 1920's Pinchot served as President of the National Conservation Association, a group fighting to protect the country's natural resources and which was instrumental in alerting the nation to proposed attacks on conservation.

At forty-nine, Pinchot married a sophisticated and politically active woman. Pinchot and his new bride took his craving for politics to the polls. In 1920 he was elected Governor of Pennsylvania. After one term he left office only to return as Governor two term's later.

In the vast forests of the land of opportunity, lumbermen in the 1800's practiced only one policy, "cut and run." They skimmed off the cream, leaving behind a waste of scattered slash and eroding hillsides. About the wastefulness of lumbermen, he said:

> "I ran into the gigantic and gigantically wasteful lumbering of great Sequoias, many of whose trunks were so huge they had to be blown apart before they could be handled. I resented then, and I still resent, the practice of making vine stakes hardly bigger than walking sticks out of these greatest of living things."

Gifford Pinchot began his career by publicly voicing his environmental beliefs stating that the idea of "reserves" in American forests was wrong. Pinchot, a conservationist, believed that we do not need forests which will never be used but forests that can be cut and then grown again. He wanted the cutting in forests to be regulated not stopped completely. The core of practical forestry, as preached by Pinchot, was sustained-yield management, a concept designed to maintain a constant supply of timber by insuring that annual cutting did not exceed annual growth.

As Pinchot's involvement in forestry grew, so did his beliefs about the total environmental destruction going on, and his narrowness began to broaden. One February day in 1907, while

Pinchot was riding his horse through Rock Creek Park in Washington, the environmental cause took on a whole new beginning with him.

> "Suddenly the idea flashed through my head that there was a unity in this complication—that the relation of one resource to another was not the end of the story. Here were no longer a lot of different, independent and often antagonistic questions, each on its own separate little island, as we have been in the habit of thinking. In place of them, there was one single question with many parts. Seen in this new light, all these separate questions fitted into and made up the one great central problem of the use of the earth for the good of man."

A counter movement to the destruction of the environment was at last underway and Pinchot had defined it: the use of the earth for the good of man. Pinchot was a key man in a key decade, and his leadership was crucial in persuading the American people to turn from flagrant waste of resources to programs of wise stewardship.

"It is not easy for us moderns to realize our dependence on the earth," said Pinchot. "As civilization progresses, as cities grow, as the mechanical aids to human life increase, we are more and more removed from the raw materials of human existence, and we forget more easily that the natural resources must be about us from our infancy or we cannot live at all."

A new policy was born: the use of the natural resources for the greatest good for the greatest number of people over the longest period of time. Pinchot christened the new policy "Conservation." Pinchot believed that the conservation of the natural resources was the key to the future. He believed it was the key to the safety and prosperity of the American people and all the people of the world for all time to come. He believed the very existence of the nation depended on conserving the resources which are the foundations of its life.

As a member of the Inland Waterways Commission, Pinchot became an instrumental figure in the Commission's recommendations to Congress and the country. The Commission stated that plans for the improvement of navigation in inland waterways, or for any use of the waterways in connection with interstate commerce, should take into account the purification of the waters, the development of power, the control of floods, the reclamation of lands by irrigation and drainage, and all other uses of the waters or benefits to be derived from their control. The most important of the Commission's recommendations was that any plans for the use of inland waterways should regard the streams of the country as an asset of the people; should take full account of the conservation of all resources connected with running waters; and should look to the protection of these resources from monopoly and to their administration in the interest of the people. Similar words had been written thirty years earlier by John Wesley Powell.

Pinchot believed in the extraction aspects of land conservation. To him, untrampled wilderness was a form of waste and not much thought was given to wildlife and wilderness values. His beliefs led him into a controversy by the name of Hetch Hetchy and into a battle with his long-time friend, John Muir. Hetch Hetchy Valley in Yosemite was to be dammed so as to produce hydroelectric power. Pinchot forced the commercial interests to use forests wisely while Muir wanted to bar commercial activity altogether. The valley, of course, was dammed. Pinchot, for the most part, looked on the public lands as a workshop to be managed for many purposes under a plan of balanced use. The multiple-use concept of the National Forest System pretty much sums up Pinchot's beliefs on the use of the environment. Pinchot emphasized product values and considered aesthetic values merely incidental.

Pinchot was one of the great educators of his time. He taught frugality when waste was the accepted creed. He turned his back on the race for riches and sought the higher goal of public service. When money power was king in parts of our land, he aroused in the people a sense of their own power.

Gifford Pinchot and Harry Graves published a book called *The White Pine* in 1896. The purpose of the book was to assist in making clear the real nature of forestry, in exciting an interest in the subjects with which it deals, in stimulating others to similar research, and, above all, in facilitating and hastening the general introduction of right methods of forest management. Pinchot's many contributions to saving the natural environment began with this book and with his thoughts on a systematic study of American trees.

From the time Pinchot returned to the United States, after studying silvaculture in France, his outspokenness about the new science of forestry in America contributed more to our beginning knowledge on our "use of the earth for the good of man" than almost any other individual. Pinchot, more than anyone else, brought the conservation issue face to face with the American public through politics.

The Bureau of Forestry and later renamed the United States Forest Service owes most of its success to its first Chief Forester, Gifford Pinchot. He built the System, from its infancy, into a powerful conservation and political machine which finally broke through the American people's apathy about the land to a small flame of knowledge which has continued to spread to a widespread deeply emotional tie to the land.

Pinchot helped form the Society of American Foresters in his early days in forestry. The purpose of the Society was "to further the cause of forestry in America by fostering a spirit of comradeship among foresters and interested persons; by creating opportunities for a free interchange of views upon forestry and allied subjects; and by disseminating a knowledge of the purpose and achievements of forestry." He was a master at using every ounce of energy in himself and his people for the purpose of making the conservation movement mushroom.

The word conservation began with Pinchot as did the conservation movement. It was his words, to which Roosevelt listened, that enabled laws to be passed to stop the reckless destruction of timberlands, grasslands, and waterways. It was his zealous energy which began the multiple-use concept of our National Forests so as to gain from the land, but also to repay the land. Pinchot was very clear about conserving the natural resources.

> *"Without natural resources life itself is impossible. From birth to death, natural resources, transformed for human use, feed, clothe, shelter, and transport us. Upon them we depend for every material necessity, comfort, convenience, and protection in our lives. Without abundant resources prosperity is out of reach."*

The report of the Inlands Waterways Commission is one of the great conservation documents of American history. That Commission along with The National Conservation Association, of which Pinchot served as president for a decade, are just two of the many groups to which Pinchot belonged which literally opened America's eyes and ears to the Conservation Movement and enabled citizens to become more aware of the environment around them.

The remainder of Pinchot's career was as a private forester writing and speaking on the conservation movement and staying active in the political arena. He transferred the struggle for scientific conservation of natural resources from a governmental bureau to the national political scene and conservation of natural resources became firmly imbedded in the American political tradition until Gifford Pinchot's death from leukemia on October 4, 1946.

Educationally, Pinchot helped found the Yale University School of Forestry, the first forestry school in America, which through the years has trained numerous men and women in the science of forestry. These individuals and graduates from schools of forestry in other states have done as much as any group in America to foster respect for the environment. Pinchot and his contributions continue long after his death.

ENOS MILLS, 1870-1922

Emotional Words on Conservation

"The trail compels you to know yourself and to be yourself, and puts you in harmony with the universe. It makes you glad to be living. It gives health, hope, and courage, and it extends that touch of nature which tends to make you kind." Enos Mills

On April 22, 1870 a son was born to Mr. and Mrs. Enos Mills in Fort Scott, Kansas. The son was named Enos Mills, after his father. Young Enos Mills lived with his pioneer parents until the age of fourteen. As a child, Mills worked on his parent's farm experiencing a multitude of difficult work situations. Since farm families were mostly self-sufficient all family members worked hard to keep the farm performing well.

By the time Mills had grown into a young boy he had heard his mother describe the majestic mountains of Colorado in beautiful prose, story after story. The stories enthralled him as he grew until at the age of fourteen he set out alone for the state of Colorado and a lifetime of experiences as a nature guide/writer/naturalist.

Mills traveled from Kansas to Estes Park, Colorado where he decided to homestead at the base of Long's Peak. From the moment that he chose the site of his homestead cabin until his death, it was home to him, and the dearest spot on earth. It gave him the opportunity to live in the mountains, to roam over the country, to observe without hurry the nature that he loved.

In his early years in Colorado Mills worked as a ranch hand while building his cabin. As he built he often stopped to watch the arrival of new birds or view the work of beavers, always studying nature with a burning desire to gain all the knowledge he possibly could about the nature around him. He spent a vast amount of time on grammar, history, and arithmetic, mastering the rudiments of an education he never received. He labored endlessly with penmanship and spelling as well as the ability to express himself. Next to nature, books were his second love, and he proceeded methodologically to advance his knowledge of natural history in every spare moment.

Mills' first few winters away from Kansas were spent ranching in eastern Colorado and mining in Montana. Extra time was always spent in search of knowledge about life and its many interrelationships, all the while patiently waiting until he could travel home to his cabin and the mountains he loved.

After his first ascent of Long's Peak, he saw the peak in the light of what it would mean to others. Many years before another great naturalist, John Wesley Powell, made the first ascent of Long's Peak. Mills decided he must bring people to experience it, but before that he must thoroughly prepare himself for the job by exploring the entire region of lakes, peaks, and canyons. Time after time he climbed the peak alone, climbing during clear days, calm days, stormy days, by moonlight, and in the darkest of nights. Mills knew he must know the area like it was part of him and be able to speak and write about it in a scholarly, intellectual manner. Realizing the area had several glaciers, he took the opportunity to study the movements and workings of glaciers with personnel involved in a United States Geological Survey expedition. Mills continually read information available to him in order to become knowledgeable about all areas before bringing people to experience the wonders of nature.

The profession of mining was one of the possibilities available to Mills, since guiding could not take place year around. But mining to Mills did not afford the opportunity for the greatest development. The influences of nature made the stronger appeal. Even while mining he would abandon his job for weeks or even months in order to camp and explore, thereby preparing himself for a greater field of usefulness and to enrich his life.

Mills' interest in nature was not confined to his own immediate environment. He saw the mountains as a whole, each section adding interest to the other, with its variety, similarities and contrasts. He enjoyed life and all that filled it. "Play is the nearest approach to the magic fountain of youth," said Mills upon returning from one of his excursions. "The wilderness still is the supreme place to rest and play. It is doubtful if any other influence is so generally and lastingly beneficial as primeval beauty, where people and nature ever are young."

On one of his pleasure trips to the San Francisco area, Mills, then twenty years old, met a man walking by the ocean who became a dear friend and ally for life. The man was John Muir. Muir was impressed with Mills' enthusiasm for nature and urged him to systematize his already extensive knowledge of wildlife, and to learn to write and speak dynamically and convincingly in order to make others see and feel it as vividly as he did. Muir impressed Mills with the fact that, if the wilderness beauty was to be saved for future generations, America needed someone who could write and speak with authority. Muir continued by telling Mills how short a period of time it takes for the selfish few to bring about irreparable destruction and that everyone must greatly emphasize the fact that forests were being cut and burned daily. Thus, Enos Mills' talents took on a definite purpose.

After extensive traveling in the West and a year of business college in San Francisco, Mills returned to Long's Peak with the enthusiasm for becoming a great naturalist. Everywhere he went he studied glaciation, geysers, and wildlife. He continued to crave more knowledge and gain it he did.

As the years passed, Mills crowded in many activities. Time was spent in guiding, writing, speaking, and with his business venture with his Long's Peak Inn which he had developed. Summers were spent in strenuous guiding. He did more than take people to the top of Long's Peak. He delved into all phases of natural history. Mills became a nature guide of superior quality.

Mills took trips by horseback, foot, stage, train, boat, and bicycle as he traveled to deserts, plains, mountains, and seashores. Everywhere he went he gathered vital information on natural history ever striving to learn as much about the universe as any one person could know.

The importance of outdoor life and recreation became an obsession with him. He felt that the prejudices of the human mind were largely due to incorrect knowledge of natural history; to underdeveloped powers of observation; to the lack of creative imagination; and to the consequent inability to reason. He believed taking to the woods would help to remedy this unfortunate condition as well as produce long life.

In the fall of 1895, Mills made his first real forestry address. The following year, he began writing for newspapers and magazines on nature and life within nature. It was this same period of time, after two forest fires started by careless campers did enormous damage to areas around Long's Peak, that Mills began a program of forest conservation with a fiery determination to prevent such needless waste. Whenever opportunity afforded, he gave talks on the subject dwelling on the beauty of the primeval forests and their inspirational influences as well as their economic value. "Our Greatest Friend and Most Valuable Resource—The Forest" became his constant theme. Like many reformers, he was years ahead of his time, in fact, he was in the vanguard of the conservation movement in the United States.

Mills continued his guiding on Long's Peak until the summer of 1906. During the previous twenty years he had climbed the peak more than forty times alone, serving 257 times as a guide. He had climbed it during every month of the year and at every hour of the day. During his guiding years he made the first winter ascent on Long's Peak and he crossed the Continental Divide from his home to Grand Lake in the middle of winter, which was also a first. He was the second person to descend the east route of Long's Peak and he did part of that on an avalanche.

For three winters, Mills occupied a very unique position as Colorado State Snow Observer for the Irrigation Department on Snowfall and Streamflow. Mills ascertained just how much of a snow reserve had been piled up in the mountain clefts at the headwaters of streams. By doing this, valuable information concerning the possibilities for irrigating during the coming summer months was given. As Snow Observer, he walked on snowshoes on the upper slopes of the snowy range of the Rockies from the Wyoming border to the New Mexico border. He was the first and last person to occupy this very exciting but dangerous position.

On a tour of the East, one particular speech of Mills' opened a new chapter in his life. Part of that speech is listed below.

"Tell your people that if they want their children's children to see the United States become what the desert countries of Western Asia are they will cut down the forests for another generation, as they are now doing. The land of the Croesus, the richest of kings, are now the abode of jackals, where they cannot find anything to eat, because Croesus and the fools like him did not preserve the forests."

The President at the time, Theodore Roosevelt, had been following Mills' tireless and independent educational program, and realized his unusual ability to reach the public. He offered Mills a post as Government Lecturer on Forestry under Chief Forester, Gifford Pinchot. Mills accepted this assignment, but at the end of the first decade of the 1900's Mills resigned as a salaried lecturer for the Forest Service realizing that he and the Forest Service differed on environmental philosophy. The battle began with the Forest Service's policy of leasing land for grazing. Little by little the Long's Peak area became despoiled and flowers were irretrievably ruined by the ruthless grazing. Mills, heartbroken over the destruction of the environment, began yet another new adventure in his life.

After Mills broke away from the Forest Service, he spared no efforts in his plea for forest conservation. He awakened general interest, not only in trees, but also in outdoor adventure, mountain climbing, and wildlife protection. He had a real ability to see Nature as a whole; to correlate the life of animals and plants; to see the relation of trees to streamflow and climate; to observe the constructive forces of geology, and to place each within the realm of human interest and economics. He wanted to share his emotions and thoughts on conservation in every corner of his state and country.

Early in 1909, he began a plan for a national park in Colorado which was to occupy his best efforts for the next several years. He had for many years been a guide and proprietor of the Long's Peak Inn and had viewed firsthand the pleasure of the visitors to the high country. He saw the time coming when private interests would take the choicest of the nation's scenic treasures unless a fight was made on behalf of the people who should be privileged to enjoy those settings. A national park was a fascinating idea and the only hope for preserving the area he loved.

Most of the territory proposed for the new park, which Mills suggested be called Estes National Park and Game Preserve, was under Forest Service supervision and was being used under their permits for lumbering and grazing. The political machine of his one-time boss, Gifford Pinchot, did not want to relinquish control of the area. For the next seven years Mills fought to bring about the creation of a national park. In 1915 the park became reality and was named The Rocky Mountain National Park. Enos Mills was almost solely responsible for the creation of the park. In 1916, the National Park Service was created and Enos Mills introduced the bill which created it.

Out of one battle he was soon involved in other battles. He was involved in the battle against transportation concessions in national parks. He believed such concessions were monopolistic and in violation of American principles and prevented people from enjoying the parks at less expense. He was also busy in getting legislation passed for the preservation of game and closed seasons on the hunting of bears.

Mills, who was married to Esther A. Burnell, in 1918, was involved in a battle with the Park Service to permit women to guide in the National Parks. His wife Esther, an excellent student of nature in her own right, did eventually become a park guide.

"This is a beautiful world and all who go out under the open sky will feel the gentle, kindly influence of Nature and hear her good tidings. The forests of the earth are the flags

of Nature. They appeal to all and awaken inspiring universal feelings. Enter the forest and the boundaries of nations are forgotten. It may be that some time an immortal pine will be the flag of a united and peaceful world."

The above quote by Enos Mills briefly describes his feelings and beliefs about the environment. He felt that being out in the wilds with nature was one of the safest and most serene places and that a climb in the mountains would develop a love for nature and strengthen one's appreciation of the beautiful world outdoors. Mills' thoughts were beautiful, but his love for nature go much deeper.

Throughout his life, Mills continually fought for conservation of scenery or the protection of wildlife. He suggests that the hunter who is always armed and killing gives his attention to game and wanders but little and enjoys less variety and fewer adventures. Mills never carried a gun throughout all his travels because of his beliefs on protecting the wildlife and his desire to visit the environment and become intimate with its inhabitants on an equal basis.

Mills talked many times about beaver and beaver colonies. He believed that a beaver colony at the source of every stream would moderate soil erosion preventing the filling of river channels, and that they also add to the picturesqueness and beauty of many scenes that erosion causes to grow ugly. He suggests that humankind will someday pay dearly for the thoughtless and almost complete destruction of the beaver.

In additional thoughts on erosion, Mills published the following paragraph in his book *Romance of Geology*.

"Soil is a magical resource. Without it, the earth would be lifeless; with its life and growth giving power to human life and all other kinds exist comfortably in a mysterious and beautiful world. The vast forests—the great splendid trees that stand like fixed pillars while generations of men pass by, the grassy plains and prairies, innumerable fields of tasselled grain all golden in the sun, the orchards, the myriads of flowers with color shining—all these grow from life-producing soil."

Mills preached that all wildlife would become friendly if not molested and that a study of its habits and customs was a happy source of mental relaxation. He said that one should take only the barest necessities into the wilds, never take a gun, and move quietly and slowly in the wilderness so as not to alarm its inhabitants. Lightness of travel would allow an individual to see more and enjoy more by freeing a person's mind to relax and become at home and intimate with the creatures of the wilds.

After a survey of forest fires in his area Mills found that most fires were started by unattended campfires. Through a program of forestry conservation he lectured on the beauty and economic value and tried to develop a widespread appreciation of trees. Although Mills did spend some time with the United States Forest Service, he eventually broke from them because of his belief that the wilds should be left for the recreational, educational, and inspirational benefits of the people and should not be used for such things as lumbering and grazing.

It was Mills' philosophy that a live flower, a live bird, or a live tree would give much more general and lasting returns than a flower plucked, a tree cut down, or a bird slain. He believed that an acquaintance with a bird, animal, or flower would develop sympathies and promote universal brotherhood. Around his inn the chipmunks, rabbits, and birds, as well as the wildflowers, were among the interesting and helpful influences of Nature which Mills wanted his guests to enjoy, and he protected them at any cost. City animals and guns were not tolerated on his premises. Mills had posted on his grounds a notice saying:

> "You can keep this region a beautiful wild garden. Spare the flowers. Thoughtless people are destroying the flowers by pulling them up by the roots or by picking too many. Neither the roots nor the leafy stalk should be taken, and flowers, if taken, should be cut, not pulled. What do you want with an armload of wildflowers?"

This was probably the first public plea for wildflowers. It took a generation for the public to accept the creed that others should be allowed to enjoy the flowers and that a selfish destruction of wilderness would only result in ultimate desolation.

Mills saw the mountains not simply as huge elevations of the earth's surface which one climbed laboriously to get a view or make a climbing record. The forests, the valleys, the streams, and the lakes were not simply places in which to hunt, trap, fish, camp, or ride through blindly. Mills viewed the out-of-doors as a natural universe whose every detail was of absorbing interest and beauty, an inexhaustible field of study refreshing to the mind and the body, and more vital in what it had to teach than all the schools in the land. But in order to study that natural universe it must exist. That is, it must have an abundance of flowers, animals, trees, lakes, and streams and only with a strict conscience of not disturbing its contents will that prevail.

Enos Mills strongly believed that people never really have much first-hand acquaintance with the elements of nature. One of his main goals in life was to arouse an interest in everyone to become more aware of nature around them. He believed that playing on peaks or plains, among trees and waterfalls, and in calms or storms was one of the surest ways of training the senses and becoming environmentally aware. He said that nature applies materials for thought and pleasantly compels thinking.

During Mills' early years in Colorado, he believed there was a great need for guides who could tell more of the mysteries and beauties of nature in one trip than could be learned by endless study of books. As more and more people took to the wilderness, he began his life-long career as a guide. He contributed more toward environmental awareness in individuals than any school or library of books could have ever given. The broad scope of his work was to have more people enjoy the recreational, educational, and inspirational benefits of the wilderness by understanding and appreciating their surroundings.

Waiting in the wilderness, that is, lingering in a spot frequently visited by wildlife was to Mills one of the easiest and most delightful ways of getting acquainted with nature and the ways of the wild. When people visited his inn, Mills would, one way or another, get people out on the trails for a walk to timberline to see the alpine flowers, or at least get them to a waterfall where they might see a wild animal feeding. He had no piano or musical contraptions in his inn because he wanted his guests to hear the music of nature. Outdoor learning was continually going on at his inn. There were always night hikes, personal stories on adventure, or talks on plant life and wildlife. Mills wanted everyone to know what life meant as an integral part of the universe and he dedicated his life to that sharing.

It was not enough for Mills to study nature firsthand and let it end there. He wanted to set down in books the things he had discovered and share those thoughts with the world. Through his numerous newspaper and magazine articles, he opened the eyes of many readers to the wonderland of nature and invited all to share those experiences with him. Some of the most beautiful words ever written are in his fifteen published books. He wrote on rivers, fossils, icebergs, glaciers, soil, trees, rocks, deserts, flowers, animals, and how his adventures related to each. Persons reading his stories could not help but be engulfed by the magnificence of the environment around them. His words are like a magnet drawing out the pioneer spirit which most all have so deeply buried. An awareness is developed which grows with every sentence and every page.

It is because of Mills' tireless contributions that America has Rocky Mountain National Park to enjoy and spend endless hours wandering through searching for answers to understand the universe, just as he did. He also helped establish Mesa Verde National Park, Glacier National Park and the National Park Service itself. He gave us playgrounds for our minds and bodies. His words on the forests of the earth give us an awareness of life.

"How happily trees have mingled with our lives! From cave to cottage, the forest has been a mother to our good race. If we should lose the hospitality of the trees and the friendship of the forest, our race too would be lost, and the desert's pale, sad sky would come to hover above a rounded, lifeless world. Friendship is the spirit of the forest."

His life and beliefs have greatly influenced our ability to view the interaction between all living things. The pioneer boy from Kansas gave us hope for people, a caring for tomorrow, and a desire to give from that which we receive. Mills had the vision to see into the future and he had the native ability to inform the world of his store-house of knowledge. He continually fought for the sacred environment to be preserved and protected for the nation. Continually pushing himself, he caught a cold and contracted pneumonia on one of his lecture tours. After a brief illness he died on September 21, 1922. Enough credit could not be given to Enos Mills' contribution to Colorado and his country. He was a prophet, a crusader, and a believer in a cause. He was a truly great naturalist.

ALDO LEOPOLD, 1886-1948

The National Speaker for Wilderness Land Ethics

"We abuse land because we regard it as a commodity belonging to us. When we see land as a community to which we belong, we may begin to use it with love and respect."

Aldo Leopold was born in Burlington, Iowa, on January 11, 1886 to two prominent German families, the Leopold's and the Starker's. Aldo's father, son of a German aristocrat who came adventuring to the New World in the 1830's, started out on the plains selling barbed wire and roller skates to farmers in Kansas and Nebraska. After marrying into the wealthy Starker family, Aldo's father founded a company for manufacturing walnut desks. Aldo Leopold was financially stable for life, but the desk business did not quite set well with his sense of being a part of the land.

Growing up in a big mansion atop Prospect Hill, Aldo Leopold early acquired his father's and grandfather's contagious sense for things free and wild. With the Mississippi River flowing below the bluffs from horizon to horizon and overhead the wingbeats of millions of migratory waterfowl following the great continental flyway, Leopold developed a love for the out-of-doors. Leopold's Grandfather Starker was a fine naturalist himself, and Leopold's father was a sportsman with ethics, who voluntarily stopped shooting waterfowl during the mating season in the spring years before it became illegal.

As a child, Leopold, going alone or with his father or brothers, often walked the railroad tracks near his home until the bluffs opened out into bottomlands abundant with wildlife where he would watch the activity for long periods of time. On occasions, he would cross the Mississippi to the duck marshes on the Illinois side, or would head west by train to the woods and fields where the quail or partridge gathered.

Leopold often thought of himself as a modern Daniel Boone because he loved to track and hunt. But this hunter was of a unique species. He would observe the game for endless hours in its environment without stalking or disturbing the animals and their habitats and even at opportune moments would study instead of shoot the wildlife.

Education for Leopold was at Lawrencerville Academy in New Jersey and in Sheffield Scientific School at Yale where he studied field ornithology and natural history. His love for the outdoors drew him to an exciting new profession just beginning at Yale University, the Yale School of Forestry, developed for studying the art and science of forestry as preached by the first Chief of the Forest Service, Gifford Pinchot.

The new forestry profession was exactly what Leopold was looking for, being a nature lover first class. When he graduated from Yale with a Master of Forestry degree in 1909, he began his first assignment with the Forest Service at the Southwestern District of the Forest Service in Albuquerque, New Mexico. He was sent to the rural town of Springerville in east-central Arizona on the edge of the Apache National Forest. He was at last on the frontier, something he had missed in Iowa by more than a generation.

Leopold thought long and hard about the pioneer experience during his years in the Southwest. He was attracted to the country, the people, and the adventure of the era. But his training as a forester and his commitment to the conservation issue made him extremely conscious of the costs involved in unrestricted private exploitation of resources. He thought the Forest Service was prepared to deal rationally with timber resources, but he was deeply concerned about overgrazed watersheds scoured by erosion; about wildlife threatened with extinction by unrestricted hunting and destruction of habitats; about the wilderness itself, destined to disappear everywhere under the thumb of mechanized man.

The seriousness of the situation brought Leopold into the public domain when he began a series of speeches and articles on conservation and its meaning to America. His main accomplishment was promoting game management techniques in the Southwest and he gained a national reputation for his policies on wildlife conservation.

The principal of "highest use," the doctrine developed by Gifford Pinchot to open up and develop producing lands, Leopold argued, would engulf all forest areas to the point of complete destruction. He demanded and got representative portions of some forests to be retained in their wild, roadless condition in order to preserve samples of the various natural environments. The Gila National Forest in southwestern New Mexico was designated as wilderness in 1924 and thus began the establishment of a nationwide system of wilderness areas. In his activist concern for watersheds, wildlife, and wilderness, Leopold was pushing the Forest Service faster than it was prepared to go. After several years with the Forest Service he was promoted to Chief of Operations in the Southwestern District and was under tremendous pressure to deal with the Forest Service's more businesslike concerns. His heart was not in office work, and in 1924, he transferred to Madison, Wisconsin, as Associate Director of the Forest Products Laboratory, the principal research unit of the Forest Service. He accepted the position with the agreement that he would become director within a year, but the director stayed on and once again he was loaded down with administrative duties.

During his time at the Madison office, Leopold wrote numerous articles on forest and wildlife conservation and took an active part in statewide efforts on conservation administration. He also hunted wildlife and discovered the Wisconsin country. John Muir had explored this very country as a boy many, many years before.

Leopold left the Forest Service in 1928 to pioneer new dimensions in conservation. With funding from the Sporting Arms and Ammunition Manufacturers Institute he undertook a two-year survey of wildlife habitats and game restoration policy in eight states of the north-central region. His research helped inaugurate a number of wildlife research projects at five universities and confirmed his position on a new approach to wildlife conservation through scientific research and habitat management.

During the early thirties, Leopold continued his research on wildlife management. During this time, his book *Game Management* was published. The book was a basic statement of the science, art, and profession of wildlife management. It is still regarded as one of the best pieces of literature ever published on wildlife management.

In 1933, he was appointed to a newly created chair position of Game Management at the University of Wisconsin, supported by a five-year grant from the Wisconsin Alumni Research Foundation. Leopold worked out of the Department of Agricultural Economics in anticipation of his work on the problems of land utilization on Wisconsin's badly deteriorated lands.

The New Deal, instigated by President Franklin D. Roosevelt, brought Leopold even more into a dramatic reorientation of the country. Projects were underway on classification and zoning of land; resettlement of families from sub-marginal farms to areas that might support productive agriculture and a self-sustaining community life; plugging of drainage ditches; construction of dikes; reflooding of marshlands for wildlife and recreation; reforestation of sandy uplands; and construction of firebreaks, lookout towers, and roads. Leopold's life even became more hectic with his writing, teaching, research and The New Deal reorientation.

Leopold viewed the heavy emphasis on environmental improvement throughout the land, but he was somewhat dismayed by how it was progressing. Clean up crews were taking out all the brush and forest duff needed for wildlife food and shelter. Fire lanes were being built which crisscrossed the land in every direction. Government conservation methods, to Leopold, no matter how extensive and how well administered, could not possibly go far enough. He began a public plea to prevent environmental deterioration maintaining that good land use management must be demonstrated. He pushed for good educational programs and demonstration projects.

Among the conservation innovations of 1934 was the State of Wisconsin's bow-and-arrow deer hunting season which Leopold had been encouraging for years. Hunting was still available but this new season made it even more of a sport resulting in less wildlife being killed. During that same year he discovered an old farm which he purchased for a hunting camp at first, but which soon turned into a second home for his family.

For Leopold, farm experiences were a slow sensitizing of people to the land and the evolution of a "sense of country." It was here that his writing took a new direction. He talked about a "land ethic" and blending people and land into one joint quest for survival. His famous book of essays on conservation, A *Sand County Almanac,* was written at his farm. The book, an environmental plea, even took a more scientific look at humanity and its environment than he had written before. Always comparing land systems, he tried critically to separate the desirable from the objectionable features of each, to disassociate sound fact from traditional assumption; and to understand more of the workings of natural mechanisms.

The farm offered space enough and time to practice the arts of wild husbandry. "A sense of husbandry," said Leopold, "is realized only when some art of management is applied to land by some person of perception." Nothing better illustrates Leopold's sense of husbandry than his planting and encouraging his pines. He sometimes planted 5,000-6,000 pines a year on his farm. Fire seemed to be a continual enemy. A campfire once got away from a trespassing hunter and burned an area of pines near Leopold's farm before it was extinguished. Soon after that incident, a much larger fire burned most of his pine plantings. An infestation of powder post beetles spread from fire-killed trees to wounded survivors and he had to cut and burn all dead and dying trees. But all was not lost for Leopold because fire opened cones of dead trees and natural reproduction took place. "The environment would take care of itself if only left alone by Homo sapiens," was a common comment of Leopold's.

Honors in the form of the presidency of societies, chairmanship of committees, and medals were many for Leopold. He served as Chairman of the Inter-American Conference on Conservation of Renewable Resources and was on the Advisory Committee on American Participation at the United Nations Scientific Conference on Conservation and Utilization of Resources.

One small test of humankind's ability to live in harmony with the environment, it seemed to Leopold, might be his capacity to maintain viable populations of wildlife. The Forest Service was prepared to deal rationally with the timber resources, but what about the overgrazed watersheds scoured by erosion; wildlife threatened with extinction; and unrestricted hunting and destruction of the habitat. Leopold could not confine his concern to the trees, nor did he believe the Forest Service should be so restrained. Wildlife was his hobby years before it became his profession and from his perspective as a forester it seemed to him that civilization need not spell the doom of wildlife anymore than forests. The conservation idea, the idea of encouraging production by essentially natural means and harvesting on a sustained-yield basis, ought to be applicable to wild game as well as to forests.

Leopold believed that the practices of clearing fields, fencing, ground-breaking, and irrigating lost more land to erosion than the person gained. While one individual was putting a new field under irrigation, another was losing an older field from floods, and a third was causing the floods through the misuse of his range. A vicious cycle costing America irretrievable soil. Leopold said the day would come when the ownership of land would carry with it the obligation to use it and protect it, with respect to erosion, so it would not be a menace to other landowners and the public.

Leopold had an intense love for the natural world, and a sensitive appreciation of the mechanisms that make the living systems succeed. His statement on conservation aptly explains his belief.

"Conservation is a state of harmony between men and land. By land is meant all the things on, over, or in the earth. Harmony with land is like harmony with a friend; you cannot cherish his right hand and chop off his left. That is to say, you cannot love game

and hate predators; you cannot conserve the waters and waste the ranges; you cannot build the forest and mine the farm. The land is one organism. Its parts, like our own parts, compete with each other and co-operate with each other. The competitions are as much a part of the inner workings as the co-operations. You can regulate them—cautiously—but not abolish them."

To Leopold, the last word in ignorance was the person who said of a plant or animal: "What good is it?" He believed that the land mechanism as a whole was good, and every part of it was good whether it was understood or not.

The idea that a single, museum-piece segment of the environment was perfectly fine was a horrible fallacy to Leopold. That belief ignored the clear dictum of history that a species must be saved in many places if it is to be saved at all. He believed a refined taste in natural objects was the knowledge needed by America.

Leopold believed that harmony with the land would never be fully achieved, any more than justice or liberty for people would be. The important thing, according to Leopold, is not to achieve, but to strive, striving being an effort of the mind as well as a disturbance of the emotions. The sadness for Leopold came from the fact that conservation is so rarely practiced by those who must extract a living from the land.

A sense of land husbandry is realized only when some art of management is applied to land by some person of perception, according to Leopold. A sense of husbandry is unknown to the outdoorsman who works for conservation with his vote rather than his hands. The tourist who buys access to his scenery misses husbandry altogether. The sportsman who hires the state, or some underling, to be his gamekeeper also misses husbandry. Leopold believed that in order to understand the land a person must work with it, feel it, and become intimate with it. Only then will a universal understanding by an individual be realized. Leopold concluded that because society must support the farmer with subsidies to raise game, that the pleasures of husbandry-in-the-wild are as yet unknown to the farmer and ourselves.

An undeveloped sanctuary is a useless waste to those without imagination, but to Leopold the most valuable part. An awareness of history was important to him and natural origins and evolution could be learned from those empty places on maps.

Mechanization in the twentieth century greatly bothered Leopold. He believed motorized transport has destroyed the sport of wilderness travel but more than that destroyed the wilderness itself. The hunter takes the factory to the woods with him by bringing fancy guns and related items. That's not hunting as a sport but mass murder according to Leopold. What chance do the animals of the woods have? A more primitive form of hunting was acceptable to Leopold, like using a bow and arrow, but not a recreational execution.

Wilderness areas for Leopold were sanctuaries for the primitive arts of wilderness travel, but mechanized recreation has left only one-tenth of the environment to wilderness. The coastlines were areas of great concern for him because of the land and water marriage, which is where much of our knowledge on an environmental ethic could be learned. He also recommended national prairie reservations to conserve that part of the land system.

Leopold believed there was still hope for a preservation of the environment but also believed there had developed a definite sickness in the land. He wrote,

> "The disappearance of plant and animal species without visible cause, despite efforts to protect them, and the irruption of others as pests despite efforts to control them, must, in the absence of simpler explanations, be regarded as symptoms of sickness in the land organism. Both are occurring too frequently to be dismissed as normal evolutionary events. In many cases we literally do not know how good a performance to expect of healthy land unless we have a wild area for comparison with sick ones."

Wild areas are a resource which can shrink but not grow. Leopold believed that the ability to see the cultural value of wilderness boiled down, in the last analysis, to a question of intellectual humility. He said it is only the scholar who understands why the raw wilderness gives definition and meaning to the human enterprise and for this reason should be saved at any cost.

Leopold believed humankind has no ethic dealing with his relation to the land, animals, and plants which grow on it. The land relation is strictly economic. A land ethic changes the role of Homo sapiens from conqueror of the land-community to plain member and citizen of it. It plies respect for his fellow-members, and also respect for the community as such. He believed humanity is not yet ready to change roles from conqueror to plain member. The obligations which arise are far too much to give. In the philosophical sense it was inconceivable to him that an ethical relation to the environment could exist without love, respect, and admiration for land, and a high regard for its value. According to Leopold, the traveler riding through Kansas who sees very little use for the Kansas flat lands does not understand the total environment and thus cares little for what becomes of it or how the land should be maintained. Leopold believed that humanity as true companion of the environment could understand, or at least would attempt to understand, that Kansas flatland is a piece of the environment which cannot be excluded if the total environment is to survive.

Education is the key to conservation according to Leopold. The objective is to teach people to see the land, to understand what they see, and enjoy what they understand. Only then will an environmental philosophy begin and ethics regarding all living things grow and develop.

Leopold said, "He who hopes for spring with upturned eye never sees a small flower. He who despairs of spring with downcast eye steps on it, unknowing. He who searches for spring with his knees in the mud finds it, in abundance."

Aldo Leopold left innumerable contributions to our knowledge about environmental concerns. His words contribute more to a sense of understanding than most anything that could ever be done. His *Sand County Almanac* is one of the best statements on conservation and environmental awareness that has ever been recorded. Below is one of his excerpts.

"I have read many definitions of what is a conservationist, and written not a few myself, but I suspect that the best one is written not with a pen, but with an axe. It is a matter of what a man thinks about while chopping, or while deciding what to chop. A conservationist is one who is humbly aware that with each stroke he is writing his signature on the face of the land."

Through a lifetime of observation and experience, of perception and husbandry, Leopold clarified his understanding of ecological processes and the fundamental values of integrity, stability, and beauty, that he saw as the basis of learning to join with nature rather than working to control and subdue it.

Leopold saw science trying for generations to classify plants and animals into good and bad species, the good being those that do more economic good than harm. To him, it was a mistake to call the issue on economic grounds, even sound ones. The basic issue goes beyond that. The question to him was whether the countryside was a livable countryside without the "bad" species. The answer was no. Once again it was this kind of intellectual, philosophical understanding which has contributed to our becoming more aware of a total universe and how it needs all parts to function properly.

Leopold brought to the world the science of relationships, which is called ecology. He continually stressed the fact that America must deal with the relations of plants and animals, their relation to soil and water, and their relation to the Homo sapiens species. He has helped us view the inner workings of nature and the environment. Without understanding there is no caring and a plain exterior often conceals hidden riches, which to perceive requires much living in and with.

Like Mills and Muir before him, Leopold postulated that to destructively devour the environment would soon leave a land with nothing left to cherish. He preached that all plant life and wildlife must be studied scientifically by researching their homes and habitats. By doing this we become more aware of why they exist.

With his approach to wildlife conservation through research and habitat management, he gave birth to the profession of wildlife management in America and is considered the father of that profession. He, more than anyone else, has been responsible for the expansion and refinement of wildlife management as it is known today, a truly great contribution to our country.

The father of wildlife management left us with a roadmap to environmental success. Leopold wrote,

> "A score of universities teach wildlife management, conduct research for bigger and better wild animal crops. However, when carried too far, this stepping-up of yields is subject to a law of diminishing returns. Very intensive management of game and fish lowers the unit value of the trophy by artificializing it. To safeguard the expensive, artificial trophy, such as a trout, the Conservation Commission feels impelled to kill all herons and terns visiting the hatchery where it was raised, and all mergansers and others inhabiting the stream in which it is released. The fisherman

feels no loss at the sacrifice of one kind of wildlife for another, but the ornithologist is ready to bite off ten-penny nails."

Leopold placed a great deal of emphasis on ecological study in his university classes and when speaking or writing environmental essays. To him studying nature was the right step toward perception of the environment and a true awareness. He greatly emphasized the fact that nature study could and should be broken into infinitely small fractions and could be done without losing its quality. He believed the weeds in a city lot conveyed the same lesson as the redwoods. Leopold deserves a great deal of credit for ecological study as it is done today.

In 1924, Aldo Leopold gained protection for a large wilderness section in the Gila National Forest in New Mexico. Soon other national forests preserved large wilderness tracts. As a result, beginning in 1929, a system of national forest primitive areas was established. Those wilderness areas give people an opportunity to see the environment before civilization crowds it out. A unique opportunity for developing an environmental awareness is offered which can be experienced in very few corners of the earth. Leopold was perceptive enough to see a land losing its roots and gave to us a small hope for the preservation of the land for the future of humankind.

Through a lifetime of observation and experience of perception and husbandry, Leopold clarified his understanding of ecological processes and the fundamental values-integrity, stability, and beauty that he saw as the basis of a land ethic. But ethical values were a guide for individual decisions, not a substitute for them, and Leopold realized this most keenly when he considered disturbing any part of the environment. He was humbly aware that any act of disturbance was like writing his name on the face of the land.

At the urging of close friends, Leopold began to seek a publisher for his conservation essays. After a succession of publishers had turned him down, a company accepted his book, *A Sand County Almanac,* in April of 1948. A few days later his life was cut short by a heart attack while fighting a grass blaze near his farm.

Aldo Leopold's passing left a large empty space in the world of conservationists. Leopold expressed his purpose in life in the foreword of his *Almanac.* "There are some who can live without wild things, and some who cannot. These essays are the delights and dilemmas of one who can-not.

RACHEL LOUISE CARSON: 1907-1964

A Strong Voice to Corporate and Political Interests

"Mankind has gone very far into an artificial world of his own creation. He has sought to insulate himself, in his cities of steel and concrete, from the realities of earth and water and the growing seed. Intoxicated with a sense of his own power, he seems to be going farther and farther into more experiments for the destruction of himself and his world. There is certainly no single remedy for this condition and I am offering no panacea. But it seems reasonable to believe — and I do believe — that the more clearly we can focus our attention on the wonders and realities of the universe about us the less taste we shall have for the destruction of our race. Wonder and humility are wholesome emotions, and they do not exist side by side with a lust for destruction." Rachel Carson

Rachel Louis Carson, a conservationist and marine biologist, was born to Maria Frazier and Robert Carson, an insurance salesman, on May 27, 1907. She was born near Springdale, Pennsylvania, on a sixty-five acre farm. Her love of nature grew yearly as she explored her farm and its natural world. As a loner Carson researched the natural world on her own. Her early years were spent reading various stories about the sea and the oceans of the earth.

Carson graduated from high school in 1925 from a school in Parnassus, Pennsylvania. She was the top student in her class of forty-five. Following high school she attended Pennsylvania College for Women. It later became Chatham University. Carson graduated *magna cum laude* in 1929. Following her Bachelor's degree she attended Johns Hopkins University where she studied zoology and genetics. She assisted Raymond Pearl in his laboratory studying rats. Her dissertation research was on the pronephros in fish and the embryonic development. The pronephros is the most basic of the three excretory organs related to kidney development. Carson completed her Master's degree in Zoology in 1932.

Carson continued at Johns Hopkins in her doctorate but was forced to leave to find work to financially support her family. Her father, Robert Carson, died in 1935. She continued her family support by caring for her elderly mother.

An aquatic biologist career with the United States Bureau of Fisheries was her first employment as a professional in her chosen field. In 1936 she became the second woman at the Bureau of Fisheries to be hired as a full-time professional. Her job title was Junior Aquatic Biologist. While at the Bureau of Fisheries she presented fifty-two seven minute weekly educational broadcasts on the aquatic life of the oceans. The broadcasts were entitled *Romance Under the Waters*. Following the broadcasts Carson began writing articles for publication on the Chesapeake Bay marine life based on her aquatic research.

The World of Waters, an essay by Carson, was published in The Atlantic Monthly, July, 1937, as *Undersea*. The essay was Carson's chronicle of what an experience of the ocean floor would be to anyone who might journey there. By 1945 Carson decided it was time for her to leave the Fish and Wildlife service and move to other environmental research areas. However, there were no jobs available for her. It was at this point that she unexpectedly discovered what DDT, an alarming new pesticide, might do to the environment. She was appointed chief editor of publications in 1949 for the Fish and Wildlife Service, but Carson's interest in DDT was thwarted by editors and she did not publish any research on the subject until 1962. Her research and writing led to a decision to pursue a career as a full-time nature writer. Carson said:

> "It is a curious situation that the sea, from which life first arose should now be threatened by the activities of one form of that life. But the sea, though changed in a sinister way, will continue to exist; the threat is rather to life itself."

Carson's book *The Sea Around Us*, published in 1951, won a National Book Award. In 1955 she completed the third volume of her sea trilogy, *The Edge of the Sea*. This early book was a revision of her first book *Under the Sea Wind*. This set of books by Carson was a sea trilogy that explored ocean life, mainly the costal ecosystems of the Eastern seaboard, from where they met land to the deepest parts of the oceans. Her book, *The Sea Around Us*, stayed on the

New York Times Best Seller List for eighty-six weeks. It won the National Book Award for nonfiction and the Burroughs Medal. She also was awarded two honorary doctorates as a result of her book. The *Sea Around Us* was developed into a documentary. However, Carson was upset with the final script saying it was "Completely untrue to the atmosphere of the book and scientifically embarrassing." Carson continued saying, "It is a cross between a believe-it-or-not and a breezy travelogue." The documentary won the 1953 Academy Award for Best Documentary Feature. Carson's reaction was to never again sell film rights to any of her writings.

In 1947 Carson decided to focus her research and writing on specific threats to the environment and became involved with the Nature Conservancy and several other groups whose mission was to protect the environment. As her research and writing grew Carson focused on the conservation of the earth and the chemical pesticides that were destroying the environment itself.

Pesticide overuse became one of Carson's main research goals. The USDA, using chlorinated hydrocarbons and organophosphates, were growing in use in an effort to eliminate fire ants. During the decade of the 1940's she also became concerned about how the military funding of science research since World War II had grown with the use of synthetic pesticides. In 1957 the American government began spraying DDT, and other pesticides mixed with fuel oil, on private land to remove the gypsy moth. Joining with the National Audubon Society, who spoke against the use of spraying programs, Carson began research on the United States government's pesticide spraying practices. Her research encompassed a four-year period of time that eventually became her basis for *Silent Spring.* In her book she shared:

> *"Why should we tolerate a diet of weak poisons, a home in insipid surroundings, a circle of acquaintances who are not quite our enemies, the noise of motors with just enough relief to prevent insanity? Who would want to live in a world which is just not quite fatal?"*

Carson's research and writing on *Silent Spring,* her most famous book, spanned several years and was finally published in 1962. The reaction of the chemical companies was immediate and powerful. However, Carson's research resulted in a reversal of the national pesticide policy. The policy instituted a national ban on DDT and other pesticides. Carson's work eventually led to the development of the Environmental Protection Agency.

Two scientific groups were involved in the pesticide debate according to Carson. One group dismissed the possible danger of pesticides because there was no final proof they were dangerous. The other scientific group was open to the debate that harm could possibly occur with pesticide spraying and were open to other methods of pest control. Also, in 1959, the Agricultural Research Service of the United States Department of Agriculture challenged Carson with a public service film entitled "Fire Ants on Trial" to counteract bad publicity. Carson said the film ignored the dangerous outcomes to humans and wildlife of using the chemicals dieldrin and heptachior as pesticides. In *Silent Spring* Carson wrote about the concern for everyone.

> *"A Who's Who of pesticides is therefore of concern to us all. If we are going to live so intimately with these chemicals eating and drinking them, taking them into the very marrow of our bones—we had better know something about their nature and their power."*

The Great Cranberry Scandal occurred during the years 1957, 58 and 59. High levels of the herbicide aminotriazole were found in the cranberry crops. Research showed that the herbicide caused cancer in lab rats and the sale of cranberries came to a standstill. During this same timeframe the National Institutes of Health connected Carson with researchers studying the large range of cancer-causing chemicals. Through her research Carson found the connection between pesticides and cancer. Investigating hundreds of cases of pesticide exposure and the human illness that followed solidified the connection to cancer.

The publication of *Silent Spring* sent shock waves through the chemical industry. Carson accused them of putting out disinformation about the impact of pesticide poisoning on humans and the environment. The central argument by Carson was the overall negative impact humans had on nature. Four chapters in *Silent Spring* regarded clear cases of human pesticide poisoning and cancer and other human illnesses that occurred. Carson foretold the extreme health consequences on humanity and all the natural world that would transpire as weakened environmental systems were impacted by the use of poisonous chemicals. Overuse of pesticides would create insect resistance and further environmental problems because of new invasive species. Carson's warning was clear.

"We stand now where two roads diverge. But unlike the roads in Robert Frost's familiar poem, they are not equally fair. The road we have long been traveling is deceptively easy, a smooth superhighway on which we progress with great speed, but at its end lies disaster. The other fork of the road—the one less traveled by—offers our last, our only chance to reach a destination that assures the preservation of the earth."

Carson received many honors for her tireless work to protect humanity and all living things. She received the Audubon Medal from the National Audubon Society. She received the Cullum Geographical Medal from the American Geographical Society. Finally, Carson was inducted into the American Academy of Arts and Letters. The environmental movement of the early 1960's was heavily influenced by Carson as well as her impact on female scientists.

The Environmental Defense Fund was created in 1967 largely because of Carson's research and writings. The Environmental Protection Agency followed up on a conflict of interest that Carson had exposed. Carson suggested that since the United States Department of Agriculture was responsible for regulating pesticides and sharing agricultural concerns that there was a conflict since the USDA didn't seem to be responsible for any negative impact on the natural world.

Carson was accused of being a communist, a peace nut, and a fanatic. One man wrote, "Kept reminding me of trying to win an argument with a woman. It can't be done." A secretary of Agriculture and leader in the Mormon Church asked, "Why is a spinster with no children concerned with genetics?" Another critic said,

"Rachel Carson doesn't write as a scientist, but as a fanatic. A defender of the cult of the balance of nature. Her book is more poisonous than the pesticides she condemns. It should be ignored. Maybe scientists

sympathize with Miss Carson's love of wildlife. Even with her mystical attachment to the balance of nature, but they fear that her emotional and inaccurate outburst may do harm by alarming the public. If one were to faithfully follow the teachings of Rachel Carson, we would return to the Dark Ages. And the insects, and diseases, and the vermin would once again inherit our Earth."

During Carson's completion of the many chapters on cancer in *Silent Spring* a malignant tumor that had metastasized was discovered in her left breast. A mastectomy was performed. Carson contracted a respiratory virus in January of 1964. Severe anemia from radiation treatments occurred and the cancer had spread to her liver. Rachel Louise Carson died of a heart attack on April 14 of 1964. She was fifty-six years old.

Rachel Louise Carson left us a legacy of ways to save ourselves and our earth from destruction. Her words did not make money for those seeking to dominate nature. Carson's words were for our hearts to contemplate and embrace. The price was courage.

"Until we have the courage to recognize cruelty for what is is— whether its victim is human or animal—we cannot expect things to be much better in this world. We cannot have peace among men whose hearts delight in killing any living creature. By every act that glorifies or even tolerates such moronic delight in killing, we set back the progress of humanity."

PART II

ENVIRONMENTAL DEGRADATION

The Present

INTRODUCTION

The naturalists' voices from the past have brought about tremendous changes in humanity's relationship with the natural world. Those early words are timeless in regard to the challenges of the alarming environmental degradation facing humankind. There has been progress with the numerous environmental issues of the twenty-first century. But, there are an increasing number of problems to solve in our quest to keep our environment healthy for all living creatures.

The overwhelming growth of our country has forced us to the edge of an unmanageable environmental crisis. Population, pollution, and land use cause more environmental degradation resulting in climate change and global warming. Our country is facing the deterioration of the environment in ways our early naturalists could never have imagined.

The destruction of ecosystems, the extinction of life forms, and the depletion of the natural resources of air, water, and land is a threat to our very existence. Environmental degradation is brought about by humanity's activity on the biophysical environment.

Greenhouse gases in our atmosphere is above the level that causes a very dangerous impact on the environment. Weather disasters are increasing. Approximately 70% of these are caused by changes in the climate. Twenty years ago the climate change caused about 50% of the weather disasters. Flooding, droughts, heavy rains, and intense storms will likely increase.

Technology has brought about the ability to extract natural resources very quickly compared to past decades and centuries. One example is the increase of deforestation. Overpopulation has consumed natural resources at a rate never experience before. Consumerism demands more commodities for human desires and comfort. Overconsumption leads to the loss of resources and further environmental degradation. The carrying capacity of excessive unsustainable consumption is beyond what the long- term carrying capacity of the natural resources can handle. Lester Brown of the Earth Policy Institute has postulated that it would take 1.5 earths to sustain our present level of consumption.

There are several environmental degradation facts that humanity must consider. They are:

Every year we extract an estimated 55 billion tons of fossil energy, minerals, metals and bio mass from the earth.

The world has already lost 80% of its forests and we are continually losing them at a rate of 375 km2 per day.

At the current rate of deforestation, 5-10% of tropical forest species will become extinct every decade.

Every hour, 1,692 acres of productive dry land become desert.

27% of our coral reefs have been destroyed. If the rate continues, the remaining coral reefs will be gone in 30 years.

We have a garbage island floating in our ocean, mostly comprised of plastics. Its size is the combination of India, Europe, and Mexico.

We are using up to 50% more natural resources than the earth can provide.

FROM THE PAST TO THE PRESENT TO THE FUTURE

<u>Climate Change and Global Warming</u>

An overwhelming number of scientists argue that climate change is real. They defend their research that shows catastrophic weather systems resulting in frequent flooding, extremes in temperatures, droughts, disastrous wildfires, and dangerous storms are the result of climate change. They also point to melting polar ice caps, damaged ecosystems, and rising sea levels which are influenced by humans, as further evidence of climate change influences. Scientists also suggest that changes in the seasons and new diseases are the result of climate change. Their research continues with the assertion that human production of greenhouse gases from carbon dioxide and methane are forcing climate change. These scientists continue with the belief that the point of no return has already passed and that the extensive destruction of the environment has pushed climate change to a place that cannot be undone.

Global warming, one of the most debated environmental issues of today, is caused by the burning of fossil fuels and the release of industries dangerous gases. A rise in atmospheric temperature has occurred as a result of these poisonous chemicals. A greenhouse effect, global dimming and a gradual rise in seal level all occur. A warmer environment has evolved over the past century as a direct result of the large quantities of greenhouse gases which have impacted the atmosphere.

Carbon dioxide, the green house gas that is most responsible for global warming, achieved a goal of which scientists are definitely not proud. The carbon dioxide emissions reached an all time high. This all time high is higher than it has ever been in at least millions of years. The fossil fuels of gas, oil, and coal are the contributors to the greenhouse gases of carbon dioxide and methane. About 81% of the energy used today comes from these fossil fuels. One of the largest users of fossil fuel is the United States.

Water and other non-refundable resources have become scarce as a result of climate change and agriculture shifting locations. This brings social conflict, people migrating, and damaged economies.

Population

The largest issue challenging the environment today is overpopulation of humans. Almost all environmental issues arise from the overpopulation of the earth. The sheer number of human beings living on planet earth has tripled in the last six decades. These unsustainable numbers impact our necessary assets of water, food and fuel. To accommodate growth more land is developed daily. Continued building has stressed the environment beyond what it can handle. The United States is not exempt from urban sprawl though over population. The staggering numbers increasingly bring about water, food, and fuel shortages in ever increasing cycles. As the population numbers increase the problems of traffic congestion, garbage, water problems, violence and crime, and lack of political stability all contribute to huge environmental issues and social destabilization.

Medical advancements in health longevity, agricultural productivity, and abundant energy have significantly increased the growing human population. The United Nations Population Division projects that the world population will reach around 9.15 billion by 2050 when it will level off. Other scholars state that by 2100 the population may possibly be 15 billion. This amounts to an approximate increase of 70 million human beings every year.

In 1958 Aldous Huxley predicted that totalitarian governments could arise as democracy decreases due to overpopulation. More restrictions on humanity are and will be necessary to manage overpopulation. The United States is based on the freedom of democracy. However, without an increasing number of rules to manage overpopulation the environmental crisis and societal issues may increase dramatically. Automobile use may be restricted. Land and water use on personal property may be further restricted in the quest to save humanity because of overpopulation.

Water

John Wesley Powell, one of our naturalists from history published *Report on the Lands of the Arid Region of the United States* in 1878. The report was a prediction of the coming water shortages in the West and Southwest. Powell stated that there simply was not enough water in the West and

Southwest to carry the high-density population coming from the East. He also clearly expressed the same issue with large-scale agriculture and its impact on the water supply. Almost a century and a half later Powell's water shortage prediction has evolved into the critical water shortage he predicted.

Access to healthy water across our country and the world is a rapidly diminishing resource. One in five human beings do not have the ability to live near safe water. Drinking water resources across the planet are less than one percent. Many households across the United States do have access to potable water. However, many experience shortages, contaminated water, and expenses for water that are almost beyond affordability. Water experts contend that water is becoming more precious than gold and oil. Water wars will increase as the need increases. Water is an increasingly economical and political resource being controlled by those in state and federal government. By 2050 approximately two-thirds of all humans will not have access to clean water. Over the past 50 years freshwater has dropped by approximately one-third.

The contamination of water is a great concern for most Americans. Research has shown the impact of clean water from urban runoff, wastewater, acid rain, and ocean dumping. Gasoline, oil, and other toxic chemicals regularly leach into our groundwater. Fertilizers, pesticides, septic systems, landfills, road salts, and hazardous waste sites contaminate our water. The disposal of any of these accidental or intentional chemicals through any body of water causes eutrophication, the species extinction and the catastrophic spread of diseases.

Flint, Michigan is a recent example of a water pollution crisis in a community that began decades ago. It began with inexpensive use of lead water lines from community sources to homes from 1901-1920. Unfortunately, what was not well known then was that these lead pipes leach lead into the water supply. The Flint, Michigan, water supply came from and was monitored by the Detroit Water and Sewage Department. The lead leaching was considered acceptable. Also, it is true that lead exposure has decreased since the 1980's. But, the acidification of water, which communities are legally responsible to regulate, increases the dissolving of lead pipes, lead solder and brass plumbing faucets. Thus, we see in Flint the beginning of what did become a crisis on humanity.

Because of financial problems and changing water sources the Flint crisis exploded. In 2014, Flint's financial issues became so dire that they switched from treated Lake Huron water from Detroit to doing their own water treatment from the Flint River in order to save $5 million dollars in a brief time. The Flint River had been a back-up source for their water for many years. A new water plant and pipeline was added at the expense of several million dollars.

By the middle of 2014 boil water advisories were sent out to the community as the complaints about odor and water taste poured in from residents. Coliform bacteria were detected in September of 2014. Aging pipes and cold weather contributed to a further breakdown in the ability to access clean and healthy water. Residents complained about the appearance, taste, and smell of the water for 18 months. At that time a Flint physician discovered that the children of Flint had highly elevated blood levels of lead in their bodies. Documents from the city stated that research had been conducted on those homes that had lead pipes entering their location and had taken action. Unfortunately, it was discovered that the city didn't know the location of the lead pipes. The Freedom of Information Act was used. The state of Michigan got involved and outrage came from the halls of the federal government.

Flint, Michigan, is an example of how and why a city experienced an extensive water crisis in the twenty-first century. Aging water pipes, lack of oversight, financial instability, and city management brought about a perfect storm of water problems. Flint is only one city's example across the United States. It can happen anywhere and does.

Another example comes from Western Kansas where the aquifers are being pumped dry and the national problem of decreasing groundwater levels are at a critical stage. The Ogallala Aquifer, which is under eight states in the Midwest, including Kansas, provides water for the farming economies of corn, wheat and cattle. Each year more wells are going dry as the level of the Ogallala is lowered. In some areas of Western Kansas, the underground water has been depleted and irrigation is no longer possible.

As more water is pumped from the Ogallala it has reached the critical stage of not being able to replenish itself. This depletion of aquifers is becoming more and more common across the United States as the water is pumped out and an aquifer cannot replenish itself.

An analysis of the measurements of more than 32,000 wells over twenty years found that approximately two-thirds of those wells have caused major water shortages across the country. The water levels of these wells have declined 64 percent over these twenty years. Water tables have been lowered more than 100 feet in some areas. In the Midwest and the area of the Ogallala Aquifer over 4000 wells have shown a 13-foot drop from 1995 to the present.

Over pumping of water is widespread in agriculture today. This accounts for two-thirds of the United States fresh water supply. The cost of over pumping impacts all of society because the water utility prices. The battle for water is now fought in communities across the country whose water supplies have almost run dry. Those areas that still have the water and the water rights can hold hostage those areas that do not have enough water. In Western Kansas there are places that will run completely out of water in less than twenty-five years. Food will not be grown there. Farmers will essentially have worthless land without water to grow crops and feed cattle.

Our earth stores most of its freshwater underground. Aquifers like the Ogallala hold water in sand, clay, and in those underground spaces. Without water those areas collapse and our earth is changed.

Food

The availability of food and the safety of food products is a national concern. The lack of quality control, toxic contamination, antibiotics, preservatives, and hormones of food products has impacted all people. Also, other environmental issues such as climate change, overpopulation, water shortages, and land misuse contribute to food shortages and safety.

In 2013 the drought that impacted several states in America brought about the lowest number of cattle purchased since the 1950's. Milk and beef prices dramatically rose because of lack of food products. Because of a recent porcine epidemic over 6 million pigs were killed off. The price of pork rose over 13 percent. Due to ongoing drought conditions many citizens not only cannot afford meat products but now they cannot afford the price increases in fruit and vegetables. For example, because of the California drought conditions lettuce, avocados, broccoli, grapes, tomatoes, melons, peppers, berries, and corn the prices have increased from 13 to 34 percent. The U.S. Department of Agriculture stated that food prices have risen 3.5 percent and will likely go higher.

Even though people who already purchase less expensive food products try to feed themselves they are often unable to do so. People who live below the poverty line, approximately 45 million, must reduce their food expenses and consumption without actually starving.

Another crisis of the food supply comes from the world of "pollinators". These are mostly bees, but butterflies and several other insects may become extinct. Food crops are facing the loss of several billion dollars because of the shrinking pollinators. Habitat loss caused by urban development of farm land also reduces the number of pollinators. Thus, the vicious cycle of the degradation of food supply and its safety continues.

Pollution

The pollution of the environment takes numerous forms. Each is destructive it is damage to the external and internal environment where it occurs. The air all inhabitants of earth need to survive is polluted every hour of the day by a large number of causes.

Air pollution is brought about by poisons and various gasses released by burning fossil fuels and the discharge of pollutants by businesses and manufacturing plants. Water pollution, as mentioned earlier, also poisons the land.

The manner in which humans interact with the land through mechanical waste extracts the necessary supplements from soil which are needed to grow healthy crops. Mining creates long lasting environmental destruction that also causes sociological and economical issues. The leaching of heavy metals and acids into soil and water tables are often caused by carelessness.

Littering, methane emissions, overgrazing, deforestation, irrigation, construction, and industrial activities all contribute to air and land pollution and cause serious health problems with all living organisms.

Agriculture pollution occurs as a result of pesticides and fertilizers used to combat pests that invade crops. The destructive cycle continually occurs because of the need for food products humans need to survive. Pollution occurs when chemicals are used to keep away the pests that attack the crops. The chemical sprays seep into the soil and water tables which then harms the various crops and plants that we want to feed us. Agricultural and industry waste eventually moves through the soil and ground water and enters nearby bodies of water. The local water sources are already contaminated as they are used for irrigation of crops.

A constant amount of noise or even an occasional excessive amount of noise pollution causes numerous health problems. Road traffic, construction, music venues, industrial work and large group activities add to further pollution of the environment.

Indoor air pollution is also a growing concern caused by heating, cooking, and household and industrial chemicals. Carbon monoxide poisoning and the chemicals released by indoor living and work are responsible for many diseases and death.

The light pollution that humans experience is harming physical health. Humanity evolved to the cycle of day and night and the light and dark. Most human's do not truly experience the actual darkness of night. Artificial light has negatively impacted health and caused depression, obesity, diabetes, and sleep disorders.

Disrupting the sleep cycle with light pollution impacts our circadian rhythm. The hormone melatonin has antioxidant properties which assists with sleep, thyroid functioning, boosts the immune system and lowers cholesterol. However, light pollution through artificial light lowers melatonin levels in the body.

Computer screens, televisions, and many other electronic devices create a great deal of blue light which is extremely harmful to a person's sleep cycle. LED's are producers of blue light. Care has to be taken in shielding these lights and using the right light for day and night.

Waste: Household, Industrial, Nuclear

Waste from throwaway and over consumption lifestyles, medical waste, nuclear waste, electronic waste, and excessive littering have poisoned the soil and water of our living environment. Littering of our environment by disposing of debris in inappropriate locations is an enormous environmental and financial burden. The United States has become accustomed to waste as something that someone else will solve and have become numb to the serious problems it generates.

Lifestyles that continually consume without thought to the outcome are not sustainable, nor are they healthy. Fast food wrappers, consumer packaging, and cheap electronic items all litter our natural environment and landfills.

Resource consumption is at a critical level. Waste disposal from developed countries like the United States is creating a massive amount of waste, much of which ends up in waterways, oceans, and beside highways and housing areas. The disposal of this waste is a major environmental problem.

Heath care centers such as hospitals, assisted living homes, and other medical clinics produce bio-hazards from needles, syringes, blood, used sterile gloves, and even body parts. Disposal of this waste produces an environmental hazard on all living organisms. Nuclear waste has extreme health hazards associated with trying to contain it.

The waste from radioactive waste can come from commercial and industrial uses, or military and civilian reactors. Uranium mining produces radioactive waste in large volumes, also. All nuclear waste is very toxic and produces environmental dangers to any living organisms nearby. Humans, animals, and plants are at risk from waste if it not disposed of properly. Improper handling of any nuclear waste results in the leaching of heavy metals into surrounding soil and water. Even after disposal the nuclear waste still remains an environmental threat for many millennium although it is said to be safely stored.

Recycling and incineration of waste is a common practice today in the United States. However, the massive amount of waste and recycled items causes centers to become overwhelmed. Keeping up with waste disposal is almost impossible in many areas. The financial costs of incineration and recycling oftentimes are more expensive than the income produces. Subsidizing the expenses are ongoing areas of conflict in cities and counties. Other areas receive the money before a commitment to environmental health. There is a great deal of talk about saving the environment, but politics and economic issues often impedes recycling efforts. Another area of concern are the improper recycling techniques and disposal methods that continually leach toxins into the earth's soil and water. Bioaccumulation, pesticides, herbicides, DDT, endocrine disruptors, and chlorofluorocarbons are often disposed of improperly and damage the environment.

Consumerism and consumption are specifically connected to individual and industrial waste. The huge amount of consumerism and consumption in the United States in the long-term is not sustainability and continually erodes the environment for future generations.

Plastics

Plastic is used in a multitude of items and in almost every area of life from homes to hospitals. David Barnes, a researcher for the British Antarctic Survey said, "One of the most ubiquitous and long-lasting recent changes to the surface of our planet is the accumulation and fragmentation of plastics." Environmental harm occurs from the massive amount of plastic that is now used and discarded.

The beginning production of plastics in the 1940's has led the way to everyday items that seem totally essential to society. Plastics are often single-use items that are lightweight and inexpensive to make. In 2018 around 322 million tons of plastic were developed throughout the world. Regrettably, the chemicals that make plastics are possibly dangerous to humans and all living things. Some of the chemicals of plastics have been found in humans. Marine animals ingest plastic debris that injures and poisons them. Plastic waste is also used by invasive species as a method of transport to new habitats where they can invade and damage another species. Landfills are filled with plastics that can leach dangerous chemicals into the soil and water of the surrounding area.

Bisphenol A (BPS) is an organic synthetic compound used as a starting material in the development of plastic bottles and food cans. This chemical is leached into the environment through plastic containers. The U.S. Centers for Disease Control and Prevention says the majority of humans have noticeable levels of BPS in their urine. Humans with a high level of BPS have a larger rate of diabetes and heart disease. Phthalates are plastics used in vinyl flooring, wall coverings, medical items, and packaged food products. Most adults have considerable levels of phthalates in their systems.

The natural world suffers from discarded plastic because of animals becoming entangled in plastic items. More than 180 species of birds, marine mammals, and fish have been found to ingest plastic debris. Gutters, lakes, rivers, and oceans are now littered with cast off plastic either by accident or by choice.

Much of the plastic that is produced is recyclable. However, some is not reusable. Also, the massive amount of plastics to recycle often is beyond what can be handled by some companies.

Ecosystems, Endangered Species and Loss of Biodiversity

All of the natural world in a specific area is called an ecosystem. There is a relationship amongst all the natural elements. Air, water, soil, plants and animals are all connected in an ecosystem. They ecosystem may be a lake, grassland, forest, mountain tundra, or other wetlands.

New subdivisions, highways, and businesses continually move in and devour open land. Deforestation and global warming also lead to the loss of biodiversity. Ecosystems of non-human species are destroyed every time a natural area is invaded and consumed. The loss of the non-human species causes the loss of biodiversity as living systems are always interdependent and losing one leads to the loss of another and another. Destruction of ecosystems by wind, rain, earthquakes, pollution, waste, water, and over population leads to the extermination of a living species which have taken billions of years to develop. Many of these species are unknown to humans and are not considered as relevant.

However, all living things are interconnected and the loss of a species impacts our environment in ways we are not able to comprehend. It is estimated that over one hundred living species are lost each day. A loss of any living species is the loss of an abundance of living knowledge developed over millions of years of a species development. The loss is not reversible. As ecosystems are lost and exploited the rate of species loss creates more stress on the future of human existence. Human destruction of the natural environment is also the destruction of humanity.

Energy

There are two types of energy. Clean energy and dirty energy. The industrial revolution of two centuries ago began the burning of huge quantities of gas, coal, and oil to expand the economy. Research has shown that using dirty energy releases greenhouse gases through the use of burning gas, coal, and oil also brings about climate change.

Coal is by far the dirtiest and most polluting of the energies used. At least a third of carbon dioxide emissions come from burning coal. It is used to produce almost 40 per cent of the world's power.

The easy access of oil makes it possible to grow transportation at an alarming pace. It is also directly responsible for approximately one quarter of the carbon emissions that damage the climate.

Clean, renewable energy resources like wind and solar power generate electricity with little pollution. It is postulated by the Union of Concerned

Scientists that clean energy could provide approximately 40 percent of America's electricity by 2030 and perhaps 80 percent by 2050.

Fracking

Research published in *Science Advances* suggests that hydraulic fracturing may cause harm to the health of humans in that local area. Low birth weight children born to families in the local fracking area are likely to have health problems throughout life. Researchers in Pennsylvania studied 1.1 million infants from 2004 to 2013. These researchers studied infants in utero according to home addresses close to fracking areas. If a baby was born in a two-mile radius of the fracking site the baby was often less healthy and underweight. Because of newborn babies and infants living close to fracking sites they often had lower test scores, and a poorer lifestyle throughout their lives. The study says that it is probably the air pollution from the released chemicals into the air, the running diesel engines on site, and the trucks that continually enter the fracking site.

Sewage: untreated

Untreated sewage has pathogens which cause serious health problems for humans and other life forms. Health issues from sewage impacts all humans regardless of income levels or locations. Sewage often contains feces and urine pumped through the pipes coming from businesses and homes. And, often the pipes leak and break releasing untreated sewage into the ground water.

Many organisms can be found in the gastrointestinal tract of humans. These organisms end up in human waste and may be transmitted to other living beings, including humans, through untreated sewage water. Exposure may come through contaminated drinking water, getting contaminated water on skin, and through the air from inhaling water droplets.

Several diseases are caused by exposure to untreated sewage. Gastro-enteritis is an infection of the gastrointestinal tract. There may be vomiting, pain in the abdomen and possibly diarrhea. Dehydration may occur. Hepatitis is an infection of the liver and may be contracted by untreated sewage. It may look very similar to gastro-enteritis. Human skin may become yellow or jaundiced because the bile of the liver is not able to clear itself of waste products. Rashes or infected cuts may become red and swollen and have a yellow discharge. Severe pain may occur as well as a high fever.

Land Management

The continual development of land space of any size produces habitat destruction, further lack of free space, and human sprawl. Land erosion also destroys habitats and eradicates living species. Desertification is a type of land abuse in which a dry land region becomes increasingly arid to the point of losing its bodies of water as well as vegetation and wildlife. Human land use causes climate change and the result is loss of the land for any type of farming. Irrigation, methane emissions, overgrazing and monoculture also cause environmental distress as a result of intensive farming and cattle.

Deforestation of the land continues at a rapid rate. The general definition of deforestation is the clearing of green cover due to land exploitation by clear-cutting, logging and home and commercial construction. Globally, the majority of the earth's forests have been destroyed. In the United States forests are protected in many areas, but over population and several pollutions push closer to all forest areas causing harm to overall forest health. Carbon dioxide and the production of oxygen regulates rainfall and environmental temperature. Without this production rainfall may be extreme or limited. The result is a change in the environmental temperature that impacts all life.

Urban sprawl is caused by the migration of humans from city to rural land areas. Environmental health is impacted as subdivisions push further into vacant land. Biosystems are destroyed as land areas are cleared, water problems develop and water tables drop, road traffic increases causing more pollution by fossil fuels. Noise and light pollution, litter, and human waste increase environmental damage.

The Phosphorus and Nitrogen Cycles

The cycle of phosphorus and nitrogen upon the environment has an increasingly devastating impact. Approximately 120 million tons per year of nitrogen are converted into fertilizer for crops and as food additives through nitrate production. Humanity's abuse of nitrogen through technology has increased over the past decades.

Ozone Layer Depletion

Chlorine and Bromide, which are found in chlorofluorocarbons (CFC's), are toxic gases released into the environment which damage the ozone layer of the atmosphere. The ozone layer provides protection of the atmosphere and protects humanity from the harmful rays of the sun. These harmful ultra-violet radiation rays (UV's) cause numerous health problems for human beings. Many chlorofluorocarbons are banned in consumer products.

Natural Disasters

Loss of humans and other life forms and the loss of personal and commercial property caused by natural disasters have and will continue to devastate the environment. Floods, fires, earthquakes, and tornados are unpredictable and unavoidable. The overall question is how much does the destruction of the environment add to the severity of natural disasters?

Used Lead-Acid Battery recycling

Lead-acid motor vehicle batteries are installed in almost all vehicles that require a battery to function. Eventually, all of the batteries reach a point where they fail to hold energy and they need recycled. This means they become hazardous waste and a become a possible environmental problem because of the release of lead. Where are they recycled? Is it safe?

Over Fishing

Researchers estimate that by the year 2050 the seas will be barren of all fish. Over fishing of the ocean and the extreme rise in population will not meet the demands of sea food.

An example of over fishing comes from the Atlantic Cod Fishery. The Canadian Minister of Fisheries and Oceans in 1992 put a moratorium on the Atlantic Cod Fishery. The Northern Cod biomass fell to one percent of its earlier level. The Minister saw that the level of Cod was pushed to a critically low level and took action. There have been improvements in the biomass since 1992. However, at present the levels have only slowly improved. A United States report states that a failure to consider reduced resilience of cod population was probably the result of the over fishing. The increased mortality in the Gulf of Maine surface water came about from the warming of the water.

Genetic Modification

Genetic engineering using biotechnology has resulted in genetic modification. This engineering of food products possibly adds further sicknesses and poisons because of the disturbance of some very sensitive plant qualities. Animals also ingest unnatural chemicals from genetic modification and sickness and death occur.

The increased use of toxins from genetically modified food sources in order to develop insect resistant plants may also enable other life forms, including humans, to be resistant to antibiotics.

Mining: Gold and Other Minerals

The mining of gold is the largest source of mercury pollution of the environment. All mining allows the very minerals that are being brought to the surface to also bring other toxic chemicals to the earth's surface. The result is pollution of the air, water, and soil.

Ocean Acidification

Carbolic acid evolves from carbon dioxide emissions which the oceans absorb. This acidification impacts ocean life which leads to the harm of sea creatures such as the dissolving of their skeletons. The acidity of our oceans has continually increased because of carbon dioxide production. It is believed that acidity will increase by one hundred fifty percent in the next hundred years.

Nanotechnology

Nanotechnology and the future effects of nanopollution and nanotoxicology are only now being researched. Nanotechnology is used more often in consumer products and will bring many positive changes. But, a form of pollution which cannot be detected easily because of how small it is is not understood and it is unknown what the environmental impact might be.

There is waste matter and byproducts that are released during the manufacturing process of nanotechnology. Fullerenes, which are molecular spheres of carbon, are used in sports equipment and some industrial lubricants. The fullerenes become part of landfills and may contaminate the water table, soil and air.

Metals Smelting and Processing

The emission of large quantities of sulfur dioxide, hydrogen fluoride, noxious smoke fumes, gases, and other vapors continually damage the environment from the smelting of metals. Many heavy metals such as copper, cadmium zinc, lead, and nickel are also involved in the emission of toxic chemicals into the environment.

American Public Schools

School systems across the country are grappling with how to manage asbestos and mold and legionella in their walls and ceilings. HVAC systems, water treatment systems and water fountains that are old or not maintained properly cause legionella. Also, contamination from under the school buildings is occurring in many buildings. There are approximately 100,000 public schools in America. These schools are attended by over 55 million students and staff. Some schools, built between the 1950's and 1970's have hazardous polychlorinated biphenyl's (PCB's), which cause a variety of cancers. When fuel storage tanks for buses and school vehicles are located on school property there is often soil contamination because of tank leakage.

PART III

ENVIRONMENTAL IMPACT ON HUMANS:

BODY, MIND AND SPIRIT

INTRODUCTION

Just as there is severe environmental damage done to other living things, humanity also suffers great distress to its body, mind, and spirit. Humanity seems to enjoy better health than ever before. However, because of the ever-increasing population the alleged progress in physical health is now overshadowed by numerous physical health problems.

The mental health of humankind is also impacted by environmental distress. The mental ailments of anger, depression, anxiety, and extreme stress have all increased to an epidemic level. The medical professionals prescribe more pills to ease these mental traumas. Population growth has pushed humanity more closely together and personal space is more limited than ever before. The natural environment is invaded and pushed further away by the development of more housing and businesses for enlarged communities. The ability to experience the beauty of creation for emotional well-being is becoming more difficult for many people. A life of commuting to and from work in automobiles, buses, and trains leaves many people cut off from experiencing the natural environment and its healing qualities. Humanity craves emotional wellness as seen by the popularity of self-help books and workshops. Unfortunately, the natural healing of nature is sometimes only experienced through technology, pictures, and words in a book. These do not fulfill the desire for emotional healing and wellness.

As the mental and physical health of humans decline many are brought into a spiritual crisis, the third part of the human trinity. Contentment, serenity, and peacefulness are more difficult to find if a person is suffering physically and emotionally. Life circumstances, both good and bad, impact the human body in various ways. As the human body works to adapt each part of the body is influenced by every other part. Holistically the human body will work overtime to balance itself, body, mind, and spirit.

The continual search for the meaning of a person's existence has been the ongoing quest since the beginning of time. The journey is sacred. Throughout history humankind has lived, survived, and died mostly with nature. All of the natural world, including humanity, was connected and all shared it together. Humans developed beliefs and practices that defined and explained their relationship with nature. The natural world was worshiped, revered, and treated as an integral part of a person's spirituality. Early religions were developed to share the necessary connection with the natural world. Practices were symbolic of the sharing of all connections in creation. The continual movement of time in history changed humanity to a position of needing nature less and less as the world created ways to exist without embracing the natural world. Separation of humanity and nature and the sacred relationship has reached the point of conflict between the two and the lack of a healthy spiritual co-existence. The marriage of humanity and the environment and a life of spiritual well-being has reached the crisis stage.

ENVIRONMENTAL DISTRESS AND PHYSICAL HEALTH

The previous section on Environmental Degradation outlined the increasing number of environmental issues that humanity struggles to contain in an ongoing crisis of trying to maintain a healthy living space for humanity. These very same environmental conditions favor a host of health issues that arise because of the degradation. Disease vectors, invasive biota, air and water pollution, biotic and abiotic contaminants, outflows of gases, liquids, and solid waste from water treatment facilities, environmental disruptions from droughts, fires, earthquakes, and floods create conditions that favor diseases entering the human body. The lack of the basic necessities that all living things depend upon in their environment such as clean air, potable water, and healthy food to sustain their lives impacts mortality. Cancer, heart disease, and many other physical health problems are directly caused by environmental distress.

Climate Change and Global Warming

According to the Centers for Disease Control and prevention temperature and precipitation change have a major impact on the physical health of human beings. Humans have the capacity for thermoregulation up to a certain temperature level. However, weather conditions that push the threshold above or below the capacity of humans will increase health problems. During heat waves deaths occur from heat stroke and connected health issues. Respiratory disease, cardiovascular disease, and cerebrovascular disease occur during extreme temperature changes. Summer temperatures in the United States have risen. Climate change projections suggest that heat levels will increase and be more common in the coming years.

Better forecasting and heat warnings have helped. But, extreme heat events remain a cause of preventable deaths. Cities bring about urban heat islands that increase temperatures to the unsafe levels. Increased population and our aging citizens increase the risk of heat related health problems.

The opposite of the extreme heat levels occurs with the cold and snow weather patterns. The lower temperatures are expected to change with climate changes and the extreme cold temperatures may decline. Human vulnerability to extreme cold is dependent on several factors. Good housing, overall health, and age continue to be serious issues that impact people during cold extremes. Also, even though extreme cold temperatures may not be as serious for humans over time this does not counteract the increase in the heat extremes deaths and physical health problems.

An increase in heavy precipitation occurrences is expected to occur across the United States. Severe flooding causing weather-related environmental distress account for numerous deaths by drowning. The aftermath of health-related diseases related to the flooding, and the environmental destruction and diseases that follow, is a serious cause of illnesses. Waterborne diseases follow heavy precipitation. Mold contamination is caused by water left in physical structures following severe weather events. The cascading impact is the indoor air pollution that comes with the mold contamination. Humans living in a moist indoor situation have the risk of upper respiratory problems, asthma, and severe coughs. The lower respiratory infections include pneumonia and the syncytial virus that may cause a more severe case of pneumonia.

Severe drought exposes humans to other health risks. Extreme heat, dust storms, wildfires, polluted water and the dropping of adequate water available all contribute to physical health concerns. Polluted air also occurs from drought conditions and there is an increase in coccidioidomycosis which is valley fever. Fungal pathogens also transported through the air bring further health problems.

Increases in temperature can also impact the pollen release from certain plant species. The change in the time it takes for flowers to bloom and release allergenic pollen occurs more rapidly with warmer temperatures. Asthma increases with pollen releases and life styles are negatively impacted. The release of other toxic chemicals also increases with rising temperatures and allergic reactions are increased. Health facilities will see rising numbers of patients as asthma and other respiratory challenges increase with climate change.

Infectious diseases are also impacted by temperature change. Rising temperatures during the winter season allow parasites and various viruses to move into geographic areas where they previously had not been able to survive. The vectors for the spread of diseases change with climate change causing the growth of pathogens and changes to how quickly they mature and the length of infections.

Air Pollution

The Respiratory and Health Branch of the Centers for Disease Control and Prevention list the loss of lung capacity as a critical factor in early deaths. The respiratory illnesses come from both indoor and outdoor air pollution. The rising particulate matter in the air is caused by smog which is ground-level ozone matter. It is also increased by temperatures, carbon monoxide, and wildfires. Climate change as discussed earlier is a major cause of increased particulate matter resulting in further air pollution and respiratory illness.

The microclimate impact and the topography of a populated area are critical factors in the movement of air pollution. This microclimate is the climate in a small area that may be different from the surrounding populated area. The physical environment around many cities trap pollution because of the topographic barriers, such as hills. Temperatures, both warm and cold, may cause thermal inversions which spread pollutants. Often temperatures may rise with the altitude changes and the inversion stops particulate matter from rising and the pollution is left near the emission source itself and cannot be diffused into the atmosphere. Sulphur and nitrogen pollutants may be carried long distances from an original source and respiratory illnesses increase at a state and national level.

The health impact of air pollution varies across age groups. The elderly, young children, and those with chronic health problems suffer the most. Humans with asthma and other respiratory problems are also at great risk. The type of chemical pollutants and the amount of the hazardous pollution also determine the extent of the physical health impact.

Sulfur dioxide and carbon monoxide particulate matter are some of the leading causes of health issues due to air pollution. Fossil-fuel combustion combined with air stagnation often found in densely populated areas produce high levels of sulfur dioxide particulates which are inhaled. Carbon monoxide decreases the ability to move oxygen through the blood. Carboxyhemoglobin is formed in the blood and numerous cardiovascular problems occur.

Indoor air pollution impacts physical health through numerous ways and respiratory distress occurs. Asthma has increased over 75% in recent years. Because of a poorly controlled ventilation system in a building further stress occurs by the spread of dust, fireplaces, and overcrowding of the location. Chronic and acute respiratory diseases are easily spread because of larger numbers of people and this brings influenza, tuberculosis, and meningitis as possible health risks. The location of the building is also a factor if it is a vector breeding area for insects that spread disease. Also, building locations in areas prone to high moisture and flooding promote the growth of mold and thus, respiratory illnesses.

Carcinogens in our environment, such as chemical cleaners, pesticides, and artificial hormones are increasing human diseases a significant amount. These diseases often become cancerous. The Cancer Prevention Coalition has stated that cancer rates have increased around 60% in the last fifty years. Non-Hodgkin's lymphoma has almost a 100% increase. Childhood cancers have doubled. Testicular cancer has increased 300%. Breast cancer has risen 60% and brain cancer has risen almost 90%. The Cancer Prevention Coalition predicts that one in three American women will contract cancer in their lives. One out of two American men will develop cancer. A million-and-a-half Americans may be diagnosed with cancer and 43% of them will die.

Autoimmune diseases will impact about 50 million people. Autism cases have increased over 50% in recent years. Infertility rates are predicted to increase further in the coming years. Birth defects are said to affect 150,000 newborns each year. These defects have been linked to air pollution, plastics, beauty products, antibiotics, and home cleaners. There were 287 chemicals found in the umbilical cord blood of newborn babies. Breastmilk samples have shown herbicides, household cleaners, and pesticides present in the milk. Human cells mutate, and attack themselves in a contaminated environment. Environmental destruction is a factor in numerous health problems.

Research has shown that increasing rates of diabetes, high blood pressure, heart disease, SIDS, obesity and Parkinson's disease are linked to artificial infant formulas. Male and female infertility has been connected to air pollution, water pollution, paint, some waxes, exposure to lead, and pesticides.

Other Diseases

Electrical wiring, household pesticides, insecticides, and spray paint have been linked to childhood leukemia. Water pollution is linked to respiratory illnesses, hepatitis, and E-coli. Gastrointestinal and skin problems are also connected to water pollution.

Diarrheal Disease

The pathogens in water and food causes diarrheal disease. The disease transmission is caused by precipitation patterns, seasonal variations and extreme weather occurrences. The elderly and young children are the most at risk as are people who have to live with inadequate and untreated water.

Vector-Borne Diseases

The seasonal delivery of vectors such as mosquitoes, ticks and fleas are often related to land use, pest control, and issues of access to health care because of social and economic vectors. A vector is an organism that does not cause disease itself. It spreads infection by transporting pathogens from one host to another. For example, some types of mosquitoes are vectors for the malaria disease. Lyme disease, West Nile virus, plague, tularemia, Rocky Mountain spotted fever, dengue fever, Chagas disease, chikungunya, and Rift Valley viruses are several of the diseases caused by vectors increasing their travel distances. Human lifestyle and the diversity of animal hosts increases the human-vector contact rate. Also, weather unpredictability brings about consequences that continue to impact human health.

Chemical Hazards

Tobacco smoke is probably the largest airborne chemical hazard to physical health. Lung disease, lung cancer, emphysema, chronic bronchitis and disease of the heart are often caused by tobacco smoke. Non-smokers who are passively exposed to tobacco smoke are also at risk for the above illnesses. Asthma is increased with the additional sulfur dioxide, ozone and other pollutants contained in the smog which often covers larger cities.

Solid fuels, such as combustion of coal, liquid petroleum, incineration, and the combustion of any fossil fuel, contain polycyclic aromatic hydrocarbons and sulfur dioxide, dioxins, and other particulate matter. These chemical hazards impact carbon dioxide which adds to the "green house" effect. The threat to physical health from flammable materials, industrial wastes, pesticides and other carcinogens are often the causes of numerous physical health issues.

It is imperative that people have the basics of life to live. However, it is also true food production that uses pesticides and fertilizers and emits carbon emissions from the manufacturing process does release toxic chemicals that impact personal health.

Water

Drinking water is often impacted from old water lines and contaminated water from a main water source. Gastrointestinal, E-coli, polio, skin rashes, hepatitis and respiratory illnesses are connected to water contamination. Also, viral, parasitic, and bacterial illnesses such as cholera, typhoid, poliomyelitis, gastrointestinal, diarrhea, vomiting, kidney failure, reproductive failure and hepatitis are spread through water pollution. Hepatitis, a viral disease, causes damage to the liver because of contaminated water. Cryptosporidiosis, caused by the "cryptosporidium parvum," a parasite, is a disease that has the symptoms of watery bowls, diarrhea, and stomach cramps. The Entamoeba histolytica, known as the galloping amoeba, is a parasite that impacts the lining of the stomach. Chills, fever, fatigue, high fever and diarrhea are the symptoms caused by this water borne illness.

Wildfires

Droughts contribute to conditions that raise the possibility of wildfires to vulnerable high-risk areas. Exposure to smoke from wildfires cause respiratory and cardiovascular health emergencies. Respiratory infections, chronic obstructive pulmonary disease (COPD), asthma, chest pain and recurring bronchitis are related to increases in medication and emergency department admissions. Climate change increases the risk of wildfires in many forests in the United States which emit carbon monoxide, volatile organic compounds, and nitrogen oxides. These lung illnesses are connected to the death of hundreds of thousands of human beings.

Lead

Exposure to lead may cause health problems in the nervous system, which effects neurological development, and the cardiovascular system, which impacts blood pressure.

Land Pollution

Domestic waste and hazardous industrial waste contaminate soil and groundwater because of faulty disposal tactics. Short term health effects from land pollution may be headaches, nausea and vomiting, skin rash, fatigue, eye irritations, coughing, and lung problems.

Long term health effects from land pollution may involve cancers, neurological damage, respiratory problems. Soils polluted with chemicals such as gasoline and benzene may cause leukemia. Lead in the soil causes long term health problems with many children. Mercury pollution leads to liver and kidney damage.

Traffic

Accidental injuries and deaths occur because cities depend heavily on transporting people and products. The increase in the size of all cities and towns also increased traffic congestion and health problems to human beings. Approximately 500,000 individuals are killed in accidents each year. Also, at least ten or more people are injured for every person who dies in a traffic accident. Poorly maintained streets and vehicles plus dangerous driving by many individuals cause many traffic accidents. Air and noise pollution, because of the increase in traffic, causes chronic respiratory diseases, hearing problems and malignancies.

Urban Growth

The large increase in urban growth adds to the increase and spread of communicable diseases. Disease vectors may locate in urban areas and add to the increase of other diseases mainly because of the density of those living within such close proximity. Also, alcohol and drug abuse problems may increase because of the stress which comes from so many people in such close contact.

Lower Economic Locations and Environmental Racism

Those people living at a lower socioeconomic level who are many times people of color often have unhealthy environments where they live and work. Because of their lack of sufficient monetary funds, they have fewer housing and work options. Living with the exposure to toxic hazards such as chemical and smoke conditions impacts their physical health. These people of color and the poor often live within a mile of our nation's most dangerous industrial chemicals. Because of living locations, the air, water, and land pollution are more extreme for them than for those who are able to live further away from the pollution sources. Parasites and pests are also in greater abundance in poverty-stricken areas. Also, because of poor economic conditions the poor have fewer options for health care. This often leads to the ongoing spread of an individual's health conditions.

ENVIRONMENTAL DISTRESS AND MENTAL HEALTH

"Climb the mountains and get their good tidings, Nature's peace will flow into you as sunshine flows into trees. The winds will blow their own freshness into you and the storms their energy, while cares will drop off like autumn leaves." John Muir

"Mankind has gone very far into an artificial world of his own creation. He has sought to insulate himself, in his cities of steel and concrete, from the realities of earth and water and the growing seed. Intoxicated with a sense of his own power, he seems to be going farther and farther into more experiments for the destruction of himself and his world. There is certainly no single remedy for this condition and I am offering no panacea. But it seems reasonable to believe — and I do believe — that the more clearly we can focus our attention on the wonders and realities of the universe about us the less taste we shall have for the destruction of our race. Wonder and humility are wholesome emotions, and they do not exist side by side with a lust for destruction." Rachel Carson

The awareness of the numerous environmental threats often leads to depression, anxiety and overall stress. Eco-anxiety is defined as a "severe and debilitating worry related to a changing and uncertain natural environment."

Extreme weather and natural disasters often result in psychological distress. Vulnerable groups of people may have less access to resources, such as social and economic, that can assist with positive mental health. Also, many people worry about their future because of the impact environmental degradation has on them. They feel hopeless, helpless, depressed, sad, numb, scared, frustrated and filled with anger.

Those people experiencing eco-anxiety may have mental health distress because they are worrying about themselves. This is called an egoistic value. Others may worry about other people. This is called social-altruistic value. Finally, others may worry about what is happening to the natural world itself. This is called biospheric value. These three different fear-based approaches to environmental distress all involve mental anguish, but the way individuals try to cope with this anguish may lead to different approaches to dealing with the distress.

Humans have a dependence on the natural world to provide clean water, clean air, food, energy, and stable climatic conditions. The reality is that many people do not have access to some or all of these things.

Mental Health Diagnosis and Criteria Related to Environmental Distress

The following mental health diagnosis criteria are taken from the DSM-5, *The Diagnostic and Statistical Manual of Mental Disorders.* They are some of the possible clinical diagnosis that may occur because of environmental distress on an individual.

Depression

Fatigue or loss of energy; Feelings of worthlessness; Guilt; Impaired concentration; Indecisiveness; Insomnia or hypersomnia, Diminished interest or pleasure; Restlessness or feeling slowed down; Recurring thoughts of death or suicide; Significant weight loss or gain.

Anxiety

Panic; Fear; Uneasiness; Sleep problems; Cannot stay calm and still; Cold; Sweaty; Numb or tingling hands or feet; Shortness of breath; Heart palpitations; Dry mouth; Nausea; Tense muscles; Dizziness.

Prolonged Grief Disorder

Increased irritability; Numbness; Bitterness; Detachment; Preoccupation with loss.

Acute Stress Disorder

Headaches; Acne, Chronic Pain; Digestive issues; Loss of appetite or overeating; Changes in libido; Rapid heartbeat; Sweating; Difficulty concentrating; Frequent crying spells; Weight loss or gain; Difficulty sleeping.

Trauma and Stressor Related Disorders (Includes Post-Traumatic Stress Disorder)

Unwanted upsetting memories; Nightmares; Flashbacks; Emotional distress after exposure to traumatic reminders; Physical reactivity after exposure to traumatic reminders.

Avoidance of trauma-related stimuli after the trauma, in the following way(s):

Trauma-related thoughts or feelings; Trauma-related external reminders;

Negative thoughts or feelings that began or worsened after the trauma, in the following way(s): Inability to recall key features of the trauma; Overly negative thoughts and assumptions about oneself or the world; Exaggerated blame of self or others for causing the trauma; Negative affect; Decreased interest in activities; Feeling isolated; Difficulty experiencing positive affect;

Panic Disorder

Racing heartbeat or palpitations; Shortness of breath; Feeling like you are choking; Dizziness (vertigo); Lightheadedness; Nausea; Sweating or chills; Shaking or trembling; Changes in mental state, including a feeling of derealization (feeling of unreality) or depersonalization (being detached from oneself); Numbness or tingling in your hands or feet; Chest pain or tightness; Fear that you might die.

All of the above mental disorders are from the DSM-5. Also, there are several other clinical conditions that may need to be considered. Each of the areas listed below may have an impact of the clinical diagnosis, prognosis, and treatment of those disorders previously listed.

Relational Problems

The impact of environment distress of mental illness on adult partners, caregiver and child relationships, and close family relationships may include maltreatment or neglect.

Other Problems Related to Primary Support Group

This category is considered when the mental distress is associated with behavioral, affective, and cognitive issues. Withdrawal, lack of conflict resolution, and overinvolvement are examples of behavioral problems. Anger, sadness or apathy at a support group member are examples of affective issues. The chronic negative comments about a group member are examples of cognitive issues.

Abuse and Neglect

The maltreatment of a family member may also be considered when considering one of the clinical diagnosis listed earlier.

Child Maltreatment and Neglect Problems

Nonaccidental physical injury from minor bruises, fractures, and death are the result of significant distress from a family member, caregiver, or other individual.

Adult Maltreatment and Neglect Problems

Nonaccidental injury to an intimate partner may be physical or emotional.

Educational and Occupational Problems

Problems with schooling and work are often impacted by distress in the home or workplace because of any of the mental illnesses listed above. The emotional distress because of environmental issues such as poor housing, water and air pollution, and severe weather disturbances easily contribute to school and work problems.

Housing and Economic Problems

Homelessness, inadequate housing, lack of adequate food or safe drinking water, extreme poverty, and low income all contribute to mental distress. These are often caused by environmental distress in their lives.

Problems Related to Access to Medical and Other Health Care

Where a person lives can cause numerous problems related to overall health care because of lack of nearby resources. Environmental destruction often removes access to help. The basic needs of mental health are often not affordable.

Spouse or Partner Abuse and Family Relationship Distress

It is not uncommon for any of the clinical diagnosis from the DSM V listed above to have an impact on a family system. For example, anxiety from the results of poor living conditions or a natural disaster distress family relationships. The outcome is that what may have started with one individual's anxiety begins to influence other individual's in the family. Thus, what began with anxiety about an environmental issue from one person distresses an entire family unit.

Substance-Related and Addictive Disorders

According to the DSM-5 manual, "The substance-related disorders encompass 10 separate classes of drugs: alcohol; caffeine; cannabis, hallucinogens; inhalants; opioids, sedatives, hypnotics, and anxiolytics, stimulants (amphetamine-type substances, cocaine, and other stimulants); tobacco. All drugs that are taken in excess have in common direct activation of the brain reward system, which is involved in the reinforcement of behaviors and the production of memories." As with relationship distress discussed above anxiety, depression, acute stress or any of the other clinical diagnosis may result in an addictive disorder to self-medicate the person's emotional distress.

Mental Health and Function

Nature encounters can help with mental fatigue and the restoring of a person's mental relaxation. The natural world provides space for physical activity which improves memory, learning, and cognitive functioning. Alleviating symptoms of depression, anxiety, and dementia come from outdoor nature experiences.

The ongoing experience of an urban environment often brings mental exhaustion and cognitive disturbance. The continual awareness of traffic and people push our senses to the breaking point. Reduced personal control and memory loss often are the outcomes of the hyperactivity of experiencing and living in a city. The ongoing task of sorting through all the noise and chaos while maintaining attention to important life matters is exhausting to our mental health.

Nature experiences and even scenes from nature bring us away from the noise and continual motion of a city experience. Nature allows children and adults to develop cognitive, emotional and behavioral connections. It also promotes imagination, creativity, social relationships, and cognitive development. Positive emotions come from experiencing serene natural world encounters.

The Built Environment

Where humans live and work has an enormous impact on their mental health. The architecture itself has the ability to change the behavior and mood of a person. Psychological distress comes from crowded living and working conditions, poor housing, excessive noise levels both externally and internally. The pollution of the air from toxins such as solvents, lead and mercury from hazardous materials impact aggression, anxiety, depression, the ability to regulate one's emotional state, and the ability to concentrate,

Fear, panic, sleeping problems, helplessness, and hopelessness arise as people realize they have been subjected to hazardous chemicals contained in the living and working built environment. Poor housing issues such as maintenance, hazards, heat and humidity, and defects in structure increase human emotions to dangerous levels where it seems survival is at risk. The neighborhoods where people live and work also influence mental health because of actual personal danger factors or perceived danger beliefs. The attributes of a neighborhood may provide a sense of safety. Or, it may increase a feeling of danger because of large numbers of people, the diversity of the population, and the increase in all types of pollution, such as noise, air, and water.

A learned helplessness can come about in individuals and groups because of the inability to control their surroundings. Social interaction in some neighborhoods seem uncontrollable. The presence of crime or the fear of possible crime results in an emotional crisis and illness. Often people will socially withdraw to protect themselves from emotional damage because of known and unknown fears of the built environment.

Communication with others is limited because of the actual crowding and noise levels. Aggression and unfriendly relationships may be the result of the fear of the social environment in which people reside.

More and more individuals live in high-rise building environments where there are higher levels of emotional health problems than in lower level dwellings and single homes. Alienation, isolation, loneliness, less sense of safety, powerlessness, fewer social relationships and attachments to a community are the many ways that impact people. Our virtual technology gives us less personal contact and more isolation.

Well Being and Sensory Stimulation

The stimulation we receive from touching, smelling, seeing, hearing, and tasting influences our mental well-being or our rising levels of anxiety and panic. Social isolation comes from disengaging from educational, physical and other community activities because of what our sensory stimulation tells us about our environment.

The Nurture of Nature

Outdoor green space promotes physical and thus emotional well-being. The belief that nature and the natural world provide positive mental experiences is not new. It is an ancient idea that earlier generations of people, such as our naturalists, believed true. A close relationship with the natural world provides a connection with and deep sense of belonging that increases our emotional wellness across time and all people. Philosophy, poetry, and religion have described the function that nature provides for wellness and positive mental health. There is an instinctual desire to connect with nature.

Biophilia Hypothesis (BET), as introduced by Edward O. Wilson, says that individuals have an innate desire to seek connections with the natural world. There is strong desire to share the world with all life forms. Wilson says in his book *Biophilia,* "The affiliation we have with nature is rooted in our biology and genetics." Erich Fromm, the well-known social psychologist, suggested a psychological orientation to being attracted to all that is alive and vital. It is a "love of life or living systems."

Wilson suggests that humans have an attraction and positive feelings towards species organisms, habitats, and objects in their natural world. He called these "philias". The opposite of the philias are "phobias" which are fears and aversions to the environment.

Frederick Law Olmstead, the father of American Landscape Architecture and the co-designer of places like Central Park in New York, says, "Natural scenery employs the mind without fatigue and yet exercises it; tranquilizes it and yet enlivens it; and thus, through the influence of the mind over the body, gives the effect of refreshing rest and reinvigoration to the whole system."

Rachel and Stephen Kaplan in 1989 wrote an article called "The Experience of Nature: A Psychological Perspective." They suggested that there are four necessary components that a landscape must contain if it is to provide restorative effects on direct attentional capacity. These are in the natural world and are: extent and the scope of an experience and the ability to become immersed in it; being away and the escape from daily life and routines; fascination with nature that captures attention without lots of effort; and compatibility with a person's purposes and intentions toward the environment.

When an individual identifies her or himself with nature there is a sense of belonging and thus a sense of mental well-being about life.

The research of Ottosson and Grahn showed that the cumulative positive experiences of nature bring a strength to people. The natural world is an aid and remedy to individuals in emotional crisis. Mental well-being is heightened when individuals connect with the natural world that is beyond themselves. When a person experiences the natural world beyond her or his own worries, desires, fears, and personal needs the connection made brings about the elevation of the emotional state to wellness. Being aware of living in the "present" is the outcome.

A research study published in *Proceedings of the National Academy of Science* on June 30, 2015, by co-author Gretchen Daily said that "People who walked for 90 minutes in a natural area, as opposed to participants who walked in a high-traffic urban setting, showed decreased activity in the brain associated with a key factor in depression. These results suggest that accessible natural areas may be vial for mental health in our rapidly urbanizing world." The research goes on to say that "City dwellers have a 20 percent higher risk of anxiety disorders and a 40 percent higher risk of mood disorders as compared to people in rural areas."

Ecopsychology and Ecotherapy

Ecopsychology and Ecotherapy suggests that within a person's ecological unconscious is a desire to awaken environmental reciprocity. The ancient connection to the natural environment desires healing the alienation between the modern urban feeling and thinking according to Ecopsychology. Other psychotherapies focus on the healing between individuals and other people and society.

Ecofeminism insights seek to break down sexual stereotypes, particularly the masculine tendency prevalent in political power and religious dogma that desires the overpowering need to dominate everything, including nature, as if it has no right to exist. Politicians many times are only concerned about being re-elected and special needs groups who exploit the environment rather than partnering with it are considered first when it comes to the power of the office. Religions often are only concerned with personal salvation at the expense of the natural world. Mainstream religions often present the natural world as subject to humankind's will that is set rather than a continuing ongoing creation in which human's co-exist. "Replenish the Earth and subdue it" and having "dominion" over all life on earth is the mantra. Ecopsychology and the use of Ecotherapy advances the belief that there is a fundamental connection between an individual and the natural world. It has been stated that the needs of the natural world are the same as the needs of each individual and vice-versa. And, the rights of the natural world are the same as the rights of each individual.

An example of Ecotherapy from Ed Harkness, an employee of "MindFood" says in a report from *Natural England* that, "Whatever the weather, however small or urban the garden, the gardener is made mindful of the here and now. Having your hands in the dirt and repeating tasks such as weeding or planting focuses your energy and allows you the freedom to escape the normal background noise of thoughts and feelings."

Attention Restoration Theory (ART), as its originators Kaplan and Kaplan state, defines the mental well-being of the natural world and positive emotional health. ART suggests the stimuli of nature brings about restoration from mental exhaustion that comes from mental tasks.

Roger Ulrich, one of the authors of "Stress Recovery During Exposure to Natural and Urban Environments," says that "nature may allow psychophysiological stress recovery through innate, adaptive responses to attributes of natural environments such as spatial openness, the presence of pattern or structure and water features and that these features promote positive emotions related to safety and survival." Evolutionary Theory is also referred to as Stress Reduction/Recovery Theory (SRT). These theories have promoted much of the research of emotional health and the connection with nature.

ENVIRONMENTAL DISTRESS AND SPIRITUALITY

"I have come to believe that the physical destruction of the earth extends to us, too. If we live in an environment that's wounded -- where the water is polluted, the air is filled with soot and fumes, the food is contaminated with heavy metals and plastic residues, or the soil is practically dust -- it hurts us, chipping away at our health and creating injuries at a physical, psychological, and spiritual level." These are words from Wangari Maathai on the two-way connection between spirituality and environmentalism.

Wangari Maathai, a Kenyan environmental political activist and Nobel laureate, wrote further that our interaction with nature gives us a sense of the divine as our senses embrace the beauty of creation. She also said "In degrading the environment we degrade ourselves. In the process of helping the earth to heal, we help ourselves." Her environmental activism was about the sacredness of the environment.

An environmental spiritual ethic, often called "eco-spirituality" is necessary. A person's daily activities based on this ethic leads to an environmental healing that heals the earth and also heals humanity. Embracing the environment as nurturing and life-giving moves us to a loving relationship of partnership not dominator.

Defining Spirituality and Religion as they relate to the natural world is often complicated with the two words being used interchangeable. However, for the purposes of this section on Environmental Distress and Spirituality they will be separated and defined differently. Religion is the belief in a power outside a person who is called God. Spirituality is defined as power within an individual. Religions often have a strict moral code listing rights and wrongs. Spirituality is living by the laws of the universe and it is a person recognizing that she or he is more than a body and that she or he also has a soul. Spirituality is based on love and not fear as often a religion is. Spirituality allows a person to discover truth's whereas religion tells you what the truth is. Spirituality unites the world rather than separates the world through a message connectedness. Spirituality is the law of attraction in that you get what you give. Religion may say that there is always punishment and the threat of hell if you do not follow the correct message. Spirituality invites humanity to create personal stories and develop a path as she or he goes forward.

Spirituality shows us that we are not separate but connected to the natural world and all creation. It is personal and evolves over time. A person may be spiritual but not religious. Or, a person may be spiritual and religious. It is not uncommon for a person to have a deep spirituality even within a religious organization. The religious group may support the growth of a person's spirituality by having beliefs and practices that enhance spirituality. A holistic approach may result with a positive connection and freedom to choose and explore within the relationship.

The following faiths address the issue of the relationship between humankind and the natural environment:

BAHA'I

"Every created thing in the whole universe is but a door leading into His knowledge..."— Bahá'u'lláh

"When... thou dost contemplate the innermost essence of all things, and the individuality of each, thou wilt behold the signs of thy Lord's mercy in every created thing, and see the spreading rays of His Names and Attributes throughout all the realm of being.... Then wilt thou observe that the universe is a scroll that discloseth His hidden secrets, which are preserved in the well-guarded Tablet. And not an atom of all the atoms in existence, not a creature from amongst the creatures but speaketh His praise and telleth of His attributes and names, revealeth the glory of His might and guideth to His oneness and His mercy....

"And whensoever thou dost gaze upon creation all entire, and dost observe the very atoms thereof, thou wilt note that the rays of the Sun of Truth are shed upon all things and shining within them, and telling of that Day-Star's splendours, Its mysteries, and the spreading of Its lights. Look thou upon the trees, upon the blossoms and fruits, even upon the stones. Here too wilt thou behold the Sun's rays shed upon them, clearly

visible within them, and manifested by them."
('Abdu'l-Bahá, Selections from the Writings of 'Abdu'l-Bahá, p. 41-42)

The Baha'i faith says manifestations of God come through divine educators such as Abraham, Krishna, Zoroaster, Moses, Buddah, Jesus, and Muhammad. It is believed that these divine educators are all part of one religion from God. Baha'u'llah, the founder and prophet of the the Baha'i faith said, "Let your vision be world embracing."

The writings of the Baha'i faith describe the connectedness of all things. These writings chronicle the relationship and meaning of humanity as it relates to the natural world. Humanity, because of its ability to rationally understand nature can see it as sacred.

Baha'u'llah warned of materialism carried to excess and the necessity for moderation. His message was clear that humanity must come together to appreciate the sacredness of the natural world and to protect it. In order for God to reflect God's attributes it is important that the natural world and humanity unite together to continue the growth of all things. The Baha'i faith describes the evidence for the gradual evolution to the perfection of all things. Transformation occurs as the importance of the diversity of all living things show the interdependence that is necessary for society and the natural world.

The environment provides a spiritual elevation for human beings. Baha'u'llah said, "The country is the world of the soul. The city is the world of bodies." The exploitation of the natural world through materialism is the opposite of the Baha'i faith. It believes that humanity, as a part of the natural world, is here to reflect the connection needed to sustain all life.

"Wealth is a mighty barrier between the seeker and his desire," said Baha'u'llah. He went on to say that human beings should only use what they actually need. He does not say wealth is bad, but he does say that wealth should be used to assist society in forgoing unrestrained consumption of the natural world. The Baha'i faith believes that by understanding the interdependence of all of life and the freedom from squandering of unnecessary materialism that the human consciousness can further achieve its spiritual potential.

The Baha'i faith believes that the attributes of God show forth in the diversity and beauty of nature. Also, there is the belief that civilization advances itself as it becomes responsible stewards of nature.

BUDDHISM

"The Temple bell stops. But the sound keeps coming Out of the flowers." --**Basho**, 17th Century Buddhist Poet

Siddhartha Gautama, the founder of Buddhism, believed that humans and the natural world needed to be yoked together so a balanced harmony of both could be achieved. He suggested that self-indulgence and self-destruction are involved in the balanced harmony.

The four levels of the world, the existential, moral, cosmological, and the ontological, are joined together. At the existential level all beings have birth, old age, suffering and death as fundamental conditions. The Buddha's teaching at its core shares the universality of suffering. The crowning enlightenment experience is called Mahassacakka Sutta and Majjhma Nikaya. This enlightenment is a result of the path to the end of suffering. It is an act of universal compassion that the Buddha shares the existential knowledge.

The Buddhist environmental belief is that the knowledge of the universality of suffering brings compassion and empathy for all life forms. Nonviolent relief of suffering is the ethical directive by doing good rather than doing evil. Showing compassion goes beyond just sharing with human beings. It is shared with all life forms on earth. The Buddhist prayer of universal loving-kindness is, "May all beings be free from enmity; may all beings be free from injury; may all being be free from suffering; may all beings be happy."

The Buddhist notion of rebirth and karma blend the existential belief of a common condition between Buddhist cosmology and the moral dimension of all sentient living life forms. The rebirth belief connects human beings and every living animal species. The idea of karma is something in which all living life forms take part. There are traditionally three world-levels and a hierarchy of five or six different lives. The Lankavatara Sutra says that through being born a living form is kin to all domestic and wild animals, and birds born from the womb.

The first origins story from Buddhism tells of the destruction that human beings have had on creation. Greed and selfishness are the primary human characteristics that have brought environmental damage. It is the human desire to own and conquer the land that brings about conflict and chaos within the natural world. The natural processes of all life are impacted by the level of human morality. Buddhism states that humanity itself is the main reason that the environmental destruction of the earth has occurred. Humanity has caused the crisis and humanity is responsible for healing the earth. The ethics of Buddhism direct its attention to the consequences of the destruction of the natural world and believe the inclusion of plants and animals in the healing process is necessary because of their value to all living things. The Buddhist Universal Law of Causality is, "On the arising of this, that arises; on the cessation of this, that ceases."

For the Dalai Lama and other involved Buddhists their environmental ethic evolves from a sense of responsibility coming from compassion for all life. "The world grows smaller and smaller, more and more interdependent...today more than ever before life must be characterized by a sense of universal responsibility, not only...human to human but also human to other forms of life." The rejection of any sort of hierarchical dominance in the natural world is clear. Humans do not attempt to dominate each other and humans do not attempt to dominate the natural world.

Buddhadasa Bhikku, a Thai monk, exclaimed, "The entire cosmos is a cooperative. The sun, the moon, and stars live together as a cooperative. The same is true for humans, animals, trees, and the earth. When we realize that the world is mutual, interdependent, cooperative enterprise...then we can build a noble environment. If our lives are not based on this truth, then we shall perish." The traditional Buddhist focus on individual spiritual and moral conversion is adjusted to confront exploitation and environmental degradation. The Zen explanation of enlightenment shares that rivers and mountains and other natural world areas are the center of the sacred.

Buddhism teaches that since environmental problems often come from the activity of the human race then Buddhism itself, as it emphasizes the connectedness of creation, can produce a positive relationship between humanity and the natural world. The development of compassion and modesty amongst Buddhist followers may help heal the harm done to nature. The humility of humanity as it embraces the natural world brings a mutual respect and coexistence rather than a division that has historically damaged the environment and damaged humanity.

Suffering comes from the desire for attachment and control. Letting go of belief that a person must continually hold tightly a "I win and you lose" attitude about life allows for a view of existence of the common interconnection of living things. Harming another goes against the compassionate Buddhist way of living. The goal of harmony with all of life provides a healthy relationship with nature and humanity.

The broken connection between people and the natural world can be healed through the framework that Buddhism provides. A non-abusive way of interacting provides solutions to the never-ending desire to control, use, and consume.

CHRISTIANITY

"(Jesus) is the image of the invisible God, the firstborn of all creation; for in him all things in heaven and on earth were created, things visible and invisible, whether thrones or dominions or rulers or powers -- all things have been created through him and for him. He himself is before all things, and in him all things hold together. He is the head of the body, the church; he is the beginning, the firstborn from the dead, so that he might come to have first place in everything. For in him all the fullness of God was pleased to dwell, and through him God was pleased to reconcile to himself all things, whether on earth or in heaven, by making peace through the blood of his cross." Colossians 1:15-20

The Christian Bible includes both the Old and New Testaments and thus a blend of beliefs between the Jewish religion and the Christian religion. Even with a common Bible there are multiple Christian traditions that vary on the subject of the environment. However, one common theme is a Biblical view of human dominion over creation.

The Old Testament explains God's Spirit in the creation of the world. Throughout the Old and New Testaments there are numerous events of God's Spirit as a healer of all living things. Biblical expressions of the Spirit are often mentioned as water, light, fire, and wind. In the midst of God as healer there is a multidimensional relationship amongst spirituality, morality, and cosmology. The result over the millennia is the loss of interest in the sacred power of the universe and moved to a human versus environment combative approach which is ruinous to the natural world.

Stewardship of and the sacredness of the environment is often unclear in the Bible. Dominion over the earth as God's stewards is defined as human beings being "custodians" of God's earth. Dominion in Biblical terms does not mean dominate. Christianity often suggests that we take care of the environment, but it also says we must take care of our souls and be saved first. This way of teaching allows the emphasis to be placed on the individual transcended relationship with God and a devaluing of the environment. The other worldly goals that Christianity traditionally promotes suggests that the world is corrupting and the goal is to rise above it. Therefore, environmental destruction is allowed to occur even though the Old and New Testaments clearly defines creation and what humankind's part is in it as caretakers and stewards. The human centeredness of Christianity is often seen as an end in itself but also a means to eternal salvation.

The first chapter in the Old Testament says in Genesis 1:1-31, "In the beginning God created the heavens and the earth. God said, 'let there be light'; and there was light. And God saw that the light was good...And God said, 'Let there be a firmament in the midst of the waters.' And it was so...And God said, 'Let the waters under the heavens be gathered together into one place, and let the dry land appear.' And it was so...And God saw that it was good...And God said, 'Let the waters bring forth swarms of living creatures, and let birds fly above the earth...' And God saw that it was good...And God said, 'let the earth bring forth living creatures according to their kinds: cattle and creeping things and beasts of the earth...' And God saw that it was good...Then God said, 'Let us make man in our image, after our likeness, and let them have dominion over the fish of the sea, and over the birds of the air, and over the cattle, and over every creeping thing that creeps over the earth...' And God said, 'Be fruitful and multiply, and fill the earth and subdue it; and have dominion over the fish of the sea and over the birds of the air and over every living thing that moves upon the earth...' In the next chapter, Genesis 2:15, it says, "The Lord God took the man and settled him in the Garden of Eden, to cultivate and care for it."

The land is God's and is not "owned" by anyone else. As stewards of God's land human beings are to act for God for all living beings as God's caretakers. The earth is entrusted to humanity. God lives in the earth as its creator.

In 1554, John Calvin interpreted dominion to mean a responsible care and keeping that does not neglect, injure, abuse, degrade, dissipate, corrupt, mar, or ruin the earth. It is clear that Christianity has a long history of considering the natural world and how humanity needs to care for it. It is also true that Christianity has leaned toward anthropocentrism. This is the belief that humans are the most important lifeforms on earth and that human values are what sets human beings apart. Environmental ethics suggest that because of these values and beliefs humankind's actions are the basis of distress of the natural world.

The doctrine of stewardship does flow through most Christian denominations and followers do not believe in the dominance of nature approach. They do appose actions and policies that threaten a healthy environment. Christian churches are often mixed in their stewardship beliefs. Many "green" groups in churches work toward sustainability of the environment and have this as a central part of their Christian call to stewardship. Activities, liturgies, and sacramental services show respect to the divine wisdom embedded in the environment. These promote esteem for all living things, humility, and beneficence for the sacredness of earth. Christian churches may also speak out to local, state, and national government to protect biodiversity, slow down the development of urban environments, and discuss consumerism.

In Christianity, the Spirit of God (called the Holy Spirit), is at the beginning of creation and has been with humankind since then. The Spirit has been and is alive in all life forms of creation. Therefore, the indwelling of the Divine Spirit of God in all of creation is to be respected and partnered with as the healer of all of creation.

CONFUCIANISM

"Everything has beauty, but not everyone sees it. Mankind differs from the animals only by a little and most people throw that away." Confucius

There are four key elements central to Confucian thought. The first is anthropocosmic which is the triad of heaven, which is the guiding force, the earth, which is nature, and the third is humans. This element, anthropocosmic, is central to Confucianism which arose in the eleventh century. This element contrasts with the western tradition of personal salvation as it related to a divine figure.

The second key element is an organic holism of the continuity of being. The universe is seen as unified, interconnected, and interpenetrating. The belief of microcosm and macrocosm is essential to Chinese cosmology. This means everything is always interacting and this impacts everything else. Any action has an influence on other things. This belief does not have a creator god behind the universe but has an ongoing reality of a self-generating, interconnected universe. Confucianism believes there is a "continuity of being" as described by Tu Weiming, a professor and director of The Institute for Advanced Humanistic Studies.

The third key element of Confucian thought is dynamic vitalism and is the basis of the unity of reality. It is called the "ch'i" and the material force of the universe. A reciprocity between humans and natural world material force is the unifying element of the cosmos. This ch'i is the substance of life and the basis for the continuing process of change and transformation of the universe. In Confucian thought there is recognition of the cosmos and has nature always bringing new birth and new life. The continuation and interaction of life systems, mineral, vegetable, animal, and human, allows the transformation of life in which humans are called to live in harmony.

The fourth element of Confucian thought is comprehensive ethics that both humans and nature embrace. The ethics rely on the cosmological interaction of the triad of humans, earth, and heaven. Confucian thought believes that humans are biological, historical, and ethical lifeforms who need to interact with all in the complex relationships of the universe. The care for the land requires ongoing vigilance, care, and attention. Balancing the ethical nature is the cultivation of a person's ch'i through maintaining moral and physical health.

Tung Ch'ung-shu (179-104 BCE), a leading Han Confucian says that "Heaven, earth, and humans are the basis of all creatures. Heaven gives them birth, earth nourishes them and humans bring them to completion. Heaven provides them at birth with a sense of filial and brotherly love, earth nourishes them with clothing and food, and humans complete them with rites and music. The three act together as hands and feet join to complete the body and none can be dispensed with." Responsibilities are stressed over what some would say were rights. The common good is always considered higher than individual concerns.

The ethic of indebtedness to prior generations bring a responsibility to the communal well-being of the environment for generations who follow. The ethics of Confucian thought require restraint toward using up the environment. All of this adds to the political and social stability of an area. The collective memory is important as history is valued in Confucian societies.

HINDUISM

"Supreme Lord let there be peace in the sky and in the atmosphere. Let there be peace in the plant world and in the forests. Let the cosmic powers be peaceful. Let the Brahman, the true essence and source of life, be peaceful. Let there be undiluted and fulfilling peace everywhere."
Atharva Veda (Hindu)

The natural environment in Hinduism embraces the ideas of dharmic ethics or the prakti which is the material creation. The ayurveda and the vedic literature also plays a central part in environmental thinking and action in Hinduism. The social thinking of Mahatma Gandhi also is major in the environmental movement today in regard to Gandhi's teaching about social inequalities. Non-violence against the environment is also taught.

The power of the natural world in Hinduism Vedic teaching is presented by the many rituals and books that praise the earth (bhu), the atmosphere (pluvah) and the sky (sva). The gods and goddess in Hinduism also adulate the earth (Prthivi), water (Ap) and the wind (Vayu). These gods and goddesses speak to the close environmental connections in Hinduism.

In Hinduism, the tree from the environment is a symbol of the bounty given to humanity. Many references in poetic Hindu literature speak of the trees in India. Protecting forests in India has long been a part of the belief and culture.

Vedic hymns praise rivers in Hindu religious practice. The goddess of culture and learning have praised the Sarasvati river in Hinduism. Originally, the goddess Sarasvati was the personification of this body of water. Unfortunately, the Sarasvati river is now dry in India. The northern part of India has the Ganges River and is considered a goddess coming from Siva's head which is part of the Himalaya Mountain chain. The Ganges gives life to present day India. As with the dry Sarasvati river, it is unfortunate that industrial contaminants and other wastes have polluted the rivers in India.

Historically writings found in the Upanisads and Bedas often describe the Hindu life of being connected to the environment. Wilderness images and the agrarian lifestyle in these texts describe the human and natural world unification that exists. The traditions of Tantra and Samkhya, in the Hindu belief system, suggests that the natural world is real and is a powerful part of a human's life. The opposite of these traditions is in the Advaita Vedanta tradition, which adheres to the Samkhhya cosmology principles, states that a oneness transcends the natural world and that the natural world is simply an illusion.

Dharma, a doctrine in Hinduism, is the principle of cosmic order. It states that humanity must act for sake of the good of the world. This doctrine has carried on through social ecology which blends the basic needs of people to environmental policy. Because of ever increasing air and water pollution in India there is an effort by religious thinkers and environmental activists to show that Hindu tradition has and can bring greater caring about the natural environment. The sustainability factor is a major part of the discussion with the religious thinkers and activists about Hindu belief and practice.

JAINISM

"In happiness and suffering, in joy and grief, we should regard all creatures as we regard our own self. All breathing, existing, living, sentient creatures should not be slain, nor treated with violence, nor abused, or tormented, nor driven away." Yogashastra, 500 BCE

The Jaina belief system is a nontheistic religion which began in India around 800 BCE. It has existed alongside Hinduism since that time. It was founded in opposition to orthodox Brahmanism. Its religious belief is that salvation comes through striving for perfection through the process of successive lives and with no harm to any living creatures. It is a spiritual and ethical rebirth with each life. The mantra of Jainism is that the function of souls is to help one another.

There is a belief in a storied universe that has numerous lifeforms. Hell is at the bottom of the universe. Humans and all other animals are in the center region. The heavenly domain is where the gods and goddesses exist. Ascension to the Siddha Loka, another world beyond heaven and earth, is the goal of Jainism. The Siddha Loka is a place of bliss, total consciousness, and eternal energy. In order to reach this highest level is dependent on a person's relationship with all other life forms.

The five vows a person makes to reach the Siddha Loka take place in daily living in the world. They are: nonviolence, truthfulness, absence of stealing, sexual restraint, and nonpossession of worldly things. These five vows are followed so as to not harm other living creatures. If a lifeform is injured then one's karma is thickened and this blocks the furthering of liberation to reach the highest level.

The vow of truthfulness is about the interrelatedness of living beings. This truthfulness cannot help but see any suffering caused by the waste of natural resources. Studying the world's resources and understanding that things are limited is what the vow of stealing involves. This lack of stealing recognizes the need for the earthly resources to be available to future generations. Having sexual restraint is the vow that recognizes the issue of population growth. Finally, nonpossession is the vow to consider carefully acquiring material goods and what that acquisition would do to a person and the living world.

INDIGENOUS TRADITIONS

"All this was in accordance with the Lakota belief that man did not occupy a special place in the eyes of Wakan Tanka, the Grandfather of us all. I was only a part of everything that was called the world.

"Everything was possessed of personality, only differing from us in form. Knowledge was inherent in all things. The world was a library." Luther Standing Bear, Lakota, <u>Land of the Spotted Eagle</u>

In his article, "Indigenous Traditions and Ecology", John A. Grim of Yale University says, "The term indigenous is a generalized reference to the thousands of small-scale societies who have distinct languages, kinship systems, mythologies, ancestral memories, and homelands." Grim says that these traditions are made up of stories that tell of the human interaction with local bioregions. Their beliefs cannot be separated from their natural environment, language, and governance. Kinship with the environment is central to the Indigenous peoples. The agriculturists and hunters seek to uphold the environment so it will continue to provide enough for generations to come.

The Indigenous people often display a close relationship with the natural world by giving names to natural places like rivers, rocks, and trees. It provides an intimate connection with ancestors, and events of one's life.

There is also a long history of the medicines developed from roots and herbs and other living things to help in the healing of spiritual and physical ailments of these people.

The universe is often divided into heaven, earth, and the underworld within Indigenous Traditions. The understanding of humans, animals, spirits, and gods are sometimes difficult to separate since the belief system has an ongoing interaction with the universe. Animism is the concept that intelligent spirits are a part of most living things. Since spirits inhabit living things there is not a need to dominate or reshape the natural world. Harmony in the universe of living and cosmic realms is the sacred goal of Indigenous persons rather than a goal of personal salvation.

ISLAM

"O children of Adam, eat and drink, but do not be wasteful. Allah does not like prodigals!" Koran 7:31

"Allah most gracious! It is Allah who has taught the Quran. Allah has created humankind, taught humanity speech and intelligence. It is Allah who has set the sun and the moon to follow courses exactly computed. The herbs and the trees alike bow in adoration. Allah has raised the firmament high and has set up the balance of justice in order that we may not transgress due balance. So let us establish a commitment to justice and not fall short in the balance. It is Allah who has spread out the earth for Allah's creatures; the date palm and fruit trees, the corn with its stalks for fodder, all sweet smelling plants. How numerous are the favors of Allah! Can you not see?" Koran 55: 1-13

In Islam, the Koran states that there is sacredness in the natural world. It is believed that the natural world was not created by God as something random but as a truth where important knowledge can be learned from nature. Humankind is called to protect it and watch over nature. It is common in the Koran to see the language of nature being beautiful and the many parts of each day are important to consider. Humankind is to assist with the sustaining of the environment and not cause it distress.

133

In Sura (chapter) 33:72 the Koran acknowledges that there is an offer of global trusteeship that was presented by God to the Heavens, the Earth, and the Mountains, but they refused to shoulder the responsibility out of fear. Humankind decided to choose the opportunity and had the trust (amana), but they were unjust and very ignorant. The Koran's teaching states that although humankind accepted responsibility and failed that God through mercy has enabled humankind in bearing the responsibility of the amana, However, humankind has been subjected to punishment for their unbelief.

The Prophet Muhammad in the Hadith, which is the recorded words, actions, and silent approval of the Prophet, states in Sura 2:107-5:120 that God is the ultimate holder of dominion over the creation and that all things return to God and are accountable each in their own ways. Sura 6:38 says that creation itself is a vast universe of "signs" of God's power, wisdom, beneficence, and Majesty and that living species are considered to be peoples or communities.

The word "earth" comes up 453 times in the Koran. The heaven and sky are mentioned 320 times. Islam believe that the environment is not independently of value. However, they believe it gets it value from God himself. "Humans share with all animals an origin in the common substance of water and they will return to the earth from which they came. (Sura 6:59). The Koran, Sura 59:24, also says the whole creation praises God by its very being. It goes on in Sura 6:59 to say, "With Him are the keys to the treasures of the Unseen that no one knows but He. He knows whatever there is on the earth and sea. Not a leaf falls but with his knowledge: there is not a grain in the earth's shadows, not a thing, freshly green or withered, but it is inscribed in a clear record."

Islam believes that the way a person lives life on earth is also the preparation for what they call eternal life in heaven. What follows is the teaching that by compassionate caring for the environment is what humankind needs to do to prepare for the eternal life with God. It will be a perfectly balanced peaceful afterlife in the company of angels. The prophet Muhammad's teachings on the natural world are very direct. He says, "Created beings are the dependents of God, and the creature dearest unto

God is he who does most good to God's dependents," it says. Humans' good deeds therefore, "are not limited to the benefit of the human species but rather extend to the benefit of all created beings." Further, Islam follows the belief that humankind is only a manager of the earth and not an owner. A.M. Al-Damkhi, writing on Islamic environmental ethics says, "Man should not abuse, misuse or distort the natural resources as each generation is entitled benefit from them but is not entitled to own them in an absolute sense."

JUDAISM

"There is no faithfulness, no love, no acknowledgement of God in the land. There is only cursing, lying and murder, stealing and adultery; they break all bounds and bloodshed follows bloodshed. Because of this, the land mourns and all who live in it waste away; the beasts of the field and the birds of the air and the fish of the sea are dying." Hosea 4:1-4

In Judaism the literature, liturgies, and even Jewish law all have nature as a central part of the religion. The connection between God and all living things begins with the first two chapters of Genesis in the creation stories. These accounts suggest an ongoing relationship where God continually renews creation. These stories show that humans are part of the created world but also apart from it. Jewish scholars in history debate why God created human beings last. Some scholars suggest humans were created last because they were the honored guests of God and that the rest of creation was below them and made for humanity's sustenance. Other scholars say that human beings were made last so they would not be too arrogant toward the rest of creation which was created before humanity. Therefore, the creation of humans was a divine afterthought of God.

Judaism believes that all of the natural world has value and that even though human beings have the ability to misuse it for its own benefit it is reminded of the value of all creation. The question of dominion over all living things, as written in Genesis, is not interpreted by the Jewish people as complete freedom to unfairly misuse creation. The Hebrew word for "take dominion" is y'yirdu. This word comes from the same root as does "to descend" which is yarad in Hebrew. Therefore, when humankind is considered honorable there is "dominion" over the animal world. But, when

135

humankind is not honorable it descends to a lower level that the animal world and the animal world rules over humanity. The violation and abuse of the environment do not meet the definition of honorable dominion nor the highest standards of human responsibility.

In the book of Genesis, the second creation story explains humankind's relationship with creation. This is where the concept of stewardship arises. Humans (adam) are created from humus (soil). Humans are then set in the garden and told to work with it, the garden, and to watch over it. The garden is God's creation and considered God's property. The garden is not the property of humanity. A divine trust with God has the expectation that humanity is a guardian not an owner. The development of a necessary limitation by God on humanity is to guard against humankind's tendency for destroying rather than creating.

In the early agrarian society of the Hebrew people it was required that every seven years a farmer of the land, including the vineyard and olive grove, was to let the land lie fallow and unsown so the land could replenish itself for a sabbatical year. The sabbatical year is the seventh year of the seven-year agricultural cycle mandated by the Torah.

The Jewish environmental ethic is: we are only tenants on this earth. The land belongs to God. We are given permission to enjoy the Creator's abundant gifts, but we must not waste or wantonly destroy anything.

PART IV: INTO THE FUTURE

An Ending or a Beginning?

"Within this story a structure of knowledge can be established, with its human significance, from the physics of the universe and it's chemistry through geology and biology to economics and commerce and so to all those studies whereby we fulfill our role in the Earth process. There is no way of guiding the course of human affairs through the perilous course of the future except by discovering our role in this larger evolutionary process." (Thomas Berry, "The New Story," in The Dream of the Earth, 136).

"Here we might observe that the basic mood of the future might well be one of confidence in the continuing revelation that takes place in and through the earth. If the dynamics of the universe from the beginning shaped the course of the heavens, lighted the sun, and formed the earth, if this same dynamism brought forth the continents and seas and atmosphere, if it awakened life in the primordial cell and then brought into being the unnumbered variety of living beings, and finally brought us into being and guided us safely through the turbulent centuries, there is reason to believe that this same guiding process is precisely what has awakened in us our present understanding of ourselves and our relation to this stupendous process. Sensitized to such guidance from the very structure and functioning of the universe, we can have confidence in the future that awaits the human venture." (Thomas Berry, "The New Story," in The Dream of the Earth, 137).

"Perhaps the most valuable heritage we can provide for future generations is some sense of the Great Work that is before them of moving the human project from its devastating exploitation to a benign presence. We need to give them some indication of how the next generation can fulfill this work in an effective manner." (Thomas Berry, "The Great Work," in The Great Work, 7).

How we treat our environment will determine our future on earth was a message our naturalists   from history gave to us long ago. They have shown us that careful management and enlightened use of natural resources is the only way to insure a future of sufficiency for all humans. Humanity has gained much knowledge from the contributions they gave to the world. They did give us hope for the future.

John James Audubon's life was with nature and he wanted to share the emotions and beauty surrounding each inhabitant. He wanted the beauty of the wilderness to be left undisturbed and the destruction of the environment stopped. Audubon wanted his work to rekindle a stewardship of the land. Henry David Thoreau's life was part spiritual quest and part experiential living in its simplest form. His writings were models for cultural and social issues of the time. He modeled simple living. John Wesley Powell, the father of the United States Geological Survey, pushed for new land and water use control in the West. Powell gave to America a scientific understanding of the land and how to work with it. John Muir, considered the father of the National Park Service, pushed for preservation of all wilderness areas. His writings have given America hope for the wilderness as a place to go in search of a vision. Gifford Pinchot became the father of the National Forest Service. He worked with Theodore Roosevelt in introducing the issue of conservation into politics. Pinchot believed the forests should be a workshop for man and instituted the multiple-use concept of wilderness areas. Enos Mills helped establish many national parks and was a major figure in the establishment of the National Park Service. Mills, a preservationist, wanted the wilderness to be available to future generations. Aldo Leopold, the father of wildlife management believed people should be partners with the land and not conquerors. Leopold wanted a land ethic developed in people thereby enabling them to live in harmony with the land. Rachel Louise Carson was a conservationist. Her research unexpectedly led her to the role of pesticides causing environmental crisis in all living things. Carson's tireless push to ban chemical pesticides led to a policy of banning DDT and other pesticides at the national level. She then foretold the extreme health consequences on humanity and all the natural world as the result.

"So far as I can see, the future has no narrative. The future does not exist until it has become the past...If we take no thought of the future, how will we be prepared for the morrow?...And so the right thing to do today is to take thought of our future." These quotes come from Wendell Berry and his book *Our Only World.* George Santayana, a 20th century Spanish-American philosopher, used the phrase, "Those who do not know history's mistakes are doomed to repeat them." The early Naturalists did share thoughts about history's mistakes and how humanity could learn from those mistakes and positively impact the future. And, that future is now the past. The question now is are we really taking thought of our future?

Humanity has a history of wasting and abusing natural resources that are needed for the future even with the knowledge from the past of what the wasting, abusing, and overall degradation's consequences will be. Are we doing anything about it? The answer is yes. There are many positive efforts in existence that are being done to create a healthy world. Hope and fear exist at the same time. The push to save for the future and the push to exploit in the present coexist. Is it a matter of the information about humanity's mistakes not being available to everyone? Or, is it a matter of the knowledge that is available being interpreted differently? Or, is it that choices are being made, even with the knowledge, to simply disregard what is known from the past and forgoing thoughts of the future? Finally, is it that humanity has violated the natural world so severely that it is hard to envision hope because of a deepening paralysis? The answer to all the questions is "yes".

The interconnectedness of humanity and the natural world is recognized more and more. There is no humanity without the natural world. However, there is a natural world without humanity.

Therefore, the burden is on humanity to embrace and nurture the natural environment as if human lives depended on it. Because they do. Many individuals, groups, communities, states, and nations are delving deep into this world problem of saving the natural environment. The problems are extremely complex and there are not usually simple answers. Several positive things are being done at all levels. Some occur easily. Others require an extensive change in systems at many levels.

The world has continually changed. Every action, either good or bad for the environment, has consequences. Some person or some living thing is impacted. It all has a cost and it takes courage to recognize the much larger picture of where attitudes were formed. Humans develop habits of judgment on their belief systems. The belief systems provide structure, guidance, comfort, and safety. Humans lean toward what is familiar. Changing a personal internal world about helping to heal the environment may occur in an easy manner. Or, if chosen, it may come at what seems like an impossible price. It is a belief that death with occur as a result. It may be the death of a lifestyle, a family member, a friend, a job, a home, or the collapsing of an entire system which has given wealth, protection, happiness, prestige and has nurtured a person throughout life. This grief can occur at any economic level of existence. The grief isn't just about material things. It is about loss of a belief system that allowed survival.

Numerous positive changes in becoming part of the environmental healing have and are taking place at all levels. Things that are very common today are in the areas of recycling, water consumption, air quality, and developing green spaces. Recycling paper, plastic, glass, aluminum, metal, cardboard, paint, batteries, toxic chemicals, and many other items are common today. These are things most individuals, groups, and communities can do and are offered by waste companies. Individuals are helping to heal the environment in several ways. They are: using programmable thermostats; buying green power from their utility companies; using water savings shower heads and other faucet heads; fixing water leaks in faucets; using LED light bulbs; turning off lights and other appliances when not in use; reusing items such as cardboard coffee holders and sleeves; keeping cars tuned; using their own water bottles; using their own grocery bags at the market; drying clothes outside when possible; riding a bicycle; using public transportation; composting waste; working from home; using natural care products; installing solar panels; installing wind generators; and buying electric and hybrid automobiles. These are just a few of the individual ways to help with environmental healing.

Local and national businesses are comparing their planning with the environmental risks that occur because of their overall business plan. Many corporations are including financial resources to help mitigate climate damage, including paying a carbon tax on the energy tonnage they use. Other businesses and corporations are installing renewable energy sources such as solar, wind, geothermal, biomass, and hydropower energy. Wind farms with numerous generators are more prevalent by companies who sell clean energy to utility companies. Rooftops and land have solar panels and wind generators as part of the electric grid from which they draw energy. Many companies have developed energy maps which show energy efficiency goals and risks of their entire global supply chain. These businesses are recognizing that saving the environment along with social and economic growth is needed for humanity's health. Promoting sustainable markets to protect natural world resources is contributing to addressing and challenging those who damage the environment. Economic development without including a sustainable world of resources is seen as a negative business model for the future.

Companies are building with environmental investments included. Waste reduction, water conservation, clean air, and energy consumption are considered in the building process. These businesses want a healthy environment for their employees and customers and they are discovering that their financial bottom line is impacted in a positive way. With financial savings a business can pass on savings to customers and improve wages for employees. In other words, going "green" is good for business. These same businesses are installing electric car charging ports to promote the change from using fossil fuels to renewable energy sources.

Affluence and wealth often occur in an area of cities and suburbs that show how good life can be, at least according to those lucky enough to live this good life. Of course, there are many people in both areas who do not have the financial resources to live the so-called good life. It has not been uncommon for these areas to forgo energy savings measures because it might impact the comfort level of some in the affluent and poor areas. However, these populations areas are now seeing that it is financially smart to include environmental healing techniques into their population areas. Some cities and suburbs offer incentives to retrofitting buildings and houses to use less energy. Recycling and reuse events are occurring. Others are including parks, trails, and open space. The built environment is encouraged to make misused and underused areas into green areas for play, relaxation, gardens, urban agriculture projects, sharing communities, resource groups, training and teaching skills events, and overall soul healing. Community togetherness is promoted by reimagining these areas for mixed use. Healing of the natural world also includes the healing of humanity.

Technological advances are now playing a central part in slowing environmental degradation. With new technology approaches it is possible to track and identify our natural world's resources. It has been possible for many years to track and measure air quality, water quality, the tonnage of waste, the recycling industry, and several other environmental resources. It is also possible through blockchain technology to follow the complete journey of various food products from their original source to a person's kitchen. GPS tracking allows humanity to understand global food sources health and quantity on land and sea. Technology can evaluate deforestation and follow wildlife in order to present healthy possibilities for stopping dangerous habits of natural world degradation. Technology has also allowed the public sector to see and monitor the health or destruction of natural resources. The awareness of people has greatly improved through computer apps and social media sites that hold accountable those responsible for environmental degradation and the environmental insecurity of humankind on planet earth. Agriculture uses robotic farming where robots plant, weed, monitor, and predict changes in the farmed land. They use vertical farms, such as skyscrapers as a greenhouse so food can be grown throughout every season. Agriculture uses livestock biometrics so ranchers can continually monitor their livestock.

Environmental changes to protecting the natural environment have often come from a state or government level. Those services began as far back as our early naturalist's political involvement in saving the environment such as The National Park and Forest Services and the Sierra Club. Organizations begun by concerned groups of people have also arisen to combat environmental degradation. These are at the local level to the national and world level of action. Information is shared at all levels across environmental groups. This sharing of information drives the transparency of environmental destruction and small and large successes to saving the natural world. Groups join together at all levels to combat destruction. These environmental action groups also join with scientists, civil society groups, universities, city administrators, business investors, technology centers, and governments to help shape the direction of healthy, sustainable environmental solutions.

Education is also occurring at all levels about environmental destruction and environmental protection and sustainable resources. Kindergarten through twelfth grade curriculums teach the value of a sustainable world. These curriculums include the ethics and moral responsibility of all ages with ways to contribute to helping to heal the natural world. Hands on environmental activities are included in environmental curriculum. Outdoor experiences are often found in schools through day field trips and extended stay outdoor laboratory schools. The value of nature's green areas for physical, emotional, and spiritual health is built into many curriculums. Colleges have courses of study that focus on the environment. There are programs in Environmental Science and Sustainability, Outdoor Education, Outdoor Adventure, Environmental Law, Ecology, Forestry, Geology, Agriculture, Marine Biology, Botany, Oceanography, Natural Resource Management, Soil Scientists, and Zoology. Local, state, national, and world organizations have numerous opportunities to study the environment, research environmental destruction, assist in helping heal environmental areas in need, and adventure trips to experience the environment in a casual or extreme activity. Volunteerism, gardening, recreation, teaching environmental principles and ethics, and ways to improve stress levels, mental, and spiritual health are often available for all ages.

Burying the dead has also brought back a "green" burial in some areas. Environmentally friendly ways of burying people are considered as all death care options are arising. The issue is about reducing carbon emissions and stopping harmful chemicals from seeping into the soil polluting land and water. Bodies are buried in biodegradable coffins without using formaldehyde to preserve a dead body. The belief is that the body and coffin will both decompose and mix with the earth while giving nourishment to the ground. This isn't a new death practice. The history of embalming began in Egypt at about 6000 BC. Other cultures also used a form of embalming of the dead. However, throughout history it was also a common practice to not embalm a body. It wasn't until the Civil War in America that Dr. Thomas Holmes, a Captain in the Army Medical Corps, began to embalm some army officers who died in battle. Before that and after that embalming was often not a common practice. It wasn't until the 1930's that embalming became a common occurrence. The return to embalming was for sanitization, presentation, and preservation. The embalming fluids that are mostly used are formaldehyde, glutaraldehyde, and methanol which are chemicals harmful to the environment. The environmentally friendly option available today is formaldehyde free chemicals. It is still not widely used, though.

Cremation of bodies is also common place. It actually dates back about 42,000 years. However, the rise of Christianity brought an end to cremation because of the belief in the resurrection of the body. Sir Thomas Brown, in 1658, began to use cremation again because it was a sanitary precaution against disease, it reduced the price of funerals, and it would be safe from grave robbers. The number of cremations today in American is approximately 45%. Environmental arguments against cremation are the fuel contaminants used. A cremation uses about 28 gallons of fuel and releases about 540 pounds of carbon dioxide. The argument for cremation is that it takes a lot less land space in an age where grave yards are full and finding additional space is difficult.

The Natural Environments Initiative of the Harvard School of Public Health researched several areas that improve the environment and also improve human health. Providing additional green space in urban areas directly impacts mental health. People who live close to vegetation rich natural environments have improved a person's satisfaction with life. The presence of green and blue space (proximity to a costal area) also improve a person's physical health. The percentage of forest coverage has also impacted mental and physical health. Also, the Natural Environments Initiative's research has shown that the lower the area of gray space (the built environment) influences health in a positive way. The research shows clearly that the preservation of biodiversity improves personal health. Green exercise is encouraged by the nearness to a natural area. The higher levels of physical exercise show improved self-esteem, improved immune systems and less chronic disease. Cities and suburbs that allow for community gardens, rain gardens, green roofs, pocket parks, and the green use of vacant lots were also researched. They show that a hands-on approach to the environment improved emotional health, reduced stress, increased social interaction, and added healthier ways of eating. Bringing biodiversity together with the value of improving mental health, public health, and environmental health are shown and will show the best direction for the design of future building.

In his book, *Climate: A New Story*, Charles Eisenstein suggests possible changes that will help us move toward "a living world". These are possible, but may be controversial. Some of these are: Promote land regeneration through a new category of philanthropy that show how farms transition to regenerative practices.; institute a global moratorium on logging, mining, drilling, and development of all remaining primary forests, wetlands, and other ecosystems; expand the land protected in wildlife refuges and other reserves; establish new ocean marine reserves and expand existing ones; establish strict bans on driftnets and bottom trawling; ban disposable plastic bags for retail purchases; reconstitute the World Bank to serve ecological healing rather than development; promote afforestation and reforestation projects globally with an emphasis on ecologically appropriate native species; establish an eco-corps to address youth unemployment; change building codes, sanitation codes, and zoning regulations to all to allow higher density development, tiny homes, composting toilets, and wastewater treatment; reintroduce and protect keystone species such as beavers, wolves, and cougars; carry out water restoration projects worldwide through water retention landscapes; relocalize the food system and promote economic localization; apply pollution taxes to make companies internalize the social and ecological costs of toxic waste; and turn away from pesticides.

A great many positive environmental actions are being done now. Further, the future state of a healthy natural world is possible now and into the near future and beyond. There is hope because a great many visionary people from the past and the present are showing us the way. Some of it is easily done already and some of it is difficult and will require a future vision of what our world can be if changes are made. An ecological ethic and morality belief and lifestyle will be necessary. Will humanity be willing to move away from old systemic habits of environmental abuse into a caring, compassionate valuing of the place humans have in the natural world as fellow travelers and companions rather than dominators?

Are humans ready to begin the move to the new world? Or, are humans going to allow the ending of their natural world home?

KNOWING: BEING TENANTS OF PLANET EARTH

"Beyond the wall of the unreal city … there is another world waiting for you. It is the old true world of the deserts, the mountains, the forests, the islands, the shores, the open plains. Go there. Be there. Walk gently and quietly deep within it." Edward Abbey, *Beyond the Wall: Essays from the Outside*

Humankind's companionship with the natural world proceeds forward with the abundance of knowledge it has gained. The progress that has been made has greatly enhanced humanity's understanding for making an all-out effort to respect what land, tame and wild, that is still available to experience. Naturalists from history have greatly influenced the association with the environment through their dedication of comradeship with the land. Humanity has always saluted the noble bounty of nature, but at the same time abused and abandoned it. The history of the world is the story of people, the land, forests, plains, and water, continually being confronted by nature. Humankind's relationship is actually two stories. On one side is the land giving food, clothing, shelter, and inspirational feelings to the people. On the other side is the people seizing, using, and squandering the land, never giving, as in a partnership, but always taking. The early settlers in America believed themselves to be the most learned of people and the most religious. They also believed they were a divine blessing and gift to the new continent. Unfortunately, these early settlers were unleashing a disastrous abuse on an innocent natural environment.

Belatedly, humans are trying to develop a harmonious relationship. The naturalists of the past and everyone who is seeking a healthy earth today are the prime movers in the environmental critical crossroads of the present. It is through their interpretation of the past, present, and future of the environment that people can learn how to survive and thrive. The world must take their words and become more knowledgeable about environmental principles, ethics, morality and earth conscience. The forecast is simple: how we treat our environment will determine our future.

In 1968, Bill Anders, an astronaut, captured on film a beautiful picture of planet earth. The picture was taken from the window of Apollo 8. It was a picture of "Earthrise" and the beautiful blue of earth. In 2019 we may be looking forward to an "Earthset." A recent intergovernmental Panel on Climate Change said that even if a 2-degree Celsius increase occurs in the temperature of earth, as set forth by the Paris Climate threshold of 2015, the outcome will be cataclysmic. The health of humanity, the world economy, and the natural environment will be impacted severely. The next fifty years after "Earthrise" inform us what has been done and not done to save us from ourselves.

In 1973 President Nixon signed into law the Endangered Species Act. In 1974 The Safe Drinking Water Act was passed. In 1976 the Toxic Substances Control Act became law. In 1977 President Jimmy Carter presented an environmental message to Congress: "I am directing to make a one-year study of the probable changes in the world's population, natural resources and environment through the end of the century." In the 1978 Lester R. Brown wrote a book called *The Twenty Ninth Day*. In it he writes, "The French use a riddle to teach schoolchildren the nature of exponential growth. A lily pond, so the riddle goes, contains a single leaf. Each day the number of leaves doubles—two leaves the second day, four the third, eight the fourth, and so on. 'If the pond is full on the thirtieth day,' the question goes, 'at what point is it half full?' Answer: 'On the twenty-ninth day.' This global lily pond in which humanity lives may already be at least half full."

In 1980 President Jimmy Carter relocated 700 families from Love Canal because of toxic wastes deposited there. The Comprehensive Environmental Response Compensation and Liability Act, the "Superfund" legislation, directed the Environmental Protection Agency to clean up toxic waste dumps at Love Canal and Times Beach. In 1982 The United Nations World Charter for Nature passes the charter that says: "Nature shall be respected and its essential processes shall not be impaired. The genetic viability on the earth shall not be compromised, the population levels of all life forms, wild and domesticated, must be at least sufficient for their survival, and to this end necessary habitats shall be safeguarded. All areas of the earth, both land and sea, shall be subject to these principles of conservation; special protection shall be given to unique areas, to representative samples of all the different types of ecosystems and to the habitats of rare or endangered species. Ecosystems and organisms, as well as the land, marine and atmospheric resources that are utilized by man, shall be managed to achieve and maintain optimum sustainable productivity, but not in such a way as to endanger the integrity of those other ecosystems or species with which they coexist." In

1984 president Ronald Regan says in his State of the Union Address, "Preservation of our environment is not a liberal or conservative challenge, it's common sense." In 1985 The British scientist Joe Farman publishes discovery of ozone hole over Antarctica. In 1989 the Exxon Valdez oil tanker spills 11 million gallons of oil in Prince William Sound.

In 1990 the United States report on Climate Change warns that global temperature might rise 2 degrees in 35 years and recommends reducing carbon dioxide emissions. In 1991 The United Nations Antarctica treaty prohibits mining, limits pollution and protects animal species. In 1994 The United Nations Intergovernmental Panel on Climate Change report warns of severe long-term impacts from green house gas buildup. In 1992, 1,700 scientists signed the "World Scientists' Warning to Humanity." The document they wrote said that humanity and the environment are on a track for a head-on collision. In 1995 the old-growth forest logging is resumed in the Pacific Northwest. Republicans in Congress pass legislation allowing the logging to resume. President Clinton tried to block it to protect wildlife and water quality. In 1997 The Kyoto Protocol is adopted by the United States and 121 other nations, but it is not ratified by the U.S. Congress. The American industrial world predicts a disaster if carbon dioxide reductions are enforced. In 1999 The Worldwatch Institute reports that 7 out of 10 scientists believe the world is experiencing the largest mass extinction of species in world history.

In 2000 an environmental disaster in the Appalachian region of Kentucky spills 300 gallons of thick, black coal slurry sludge when a Massey Energy Company dam collapses. The Big Sandy River Tug Fork and its tributaries have over 100 miles of streams polluted and millions of fish are killed. It is one of the worst environmental disasters east of the Mississippi River. In 2001 the National Science Foundation publishes a report on Global warming that supports previous warnings by scientists. In 2002 a jury in Anniston, Alabama rules that Monsanto Chemical company was polluting the town with tons of toxic PCB's. Monsanto was liable on six counts: negligence, nuisance, suppression of the truth, trespass, wantonness and outrage.

In 2003 the George W. Bush administration compiles the most anti-environmental record of any US president in history. The Clean Air Act, the Clean Water Act, the toxic waste Superfund, the Right to Know Act, and the Marine Mammal Protection Act are all subject to abuse in this anti-environmental record. An article, "Crimes Against Nature", is published by Robert F. Kennedy Jr. saying "George W. Bush will go down in history as America's worst environmental president. In a ferocious three-year attack, the Bush administration has initiated more than 200 major rollbacks of America's environmental laws, weakening the protection of our country's air, water, public lands and wildlife. Cloaked in meticulously crafted language designed to deceive the public, the administration intends to eliminate the nation's most important environmental laws by the end of the year..."

In 2006 former U.S. vice president Al Gore releases An Inconvenient Truth a documentary that describes global warming. That same year James Hansen of the National Aeronautics and Space Administration has research that shows the earth's overall temperature has reached its highest level in 12,000 years. In 2008 scientists with the Global Climate Project estimate that the current carbon dioxide emissions will push the temperature up 11 degrees by the end of the century. In 2009 climate researchers from NOAA report that levels of carbon dioxide by 2050 would raise sea levels and bring droughts that would last 1000 years.

In 2010 the Deepwater Horizon Oil Spill occurs. In 2011 the United Nations says the world human population has reached 7 billion people. In 2012 government officials became increasingly concerned with the connection between climate change, extreme weather and how they affect public health. Also, in 2012 the United States was projected, from the International Energy Agency, to surpass Saudi Arabia in petroleum production with fracking, making the U.S. the top producer in the world. In 2013 the Mauna Loa Observatory on Hawaii's Big Island, which tracks the amount of carbon dioxide in the atmosphere, said that its readings crossed a frightening threshold. The global concentration of carbon dioxide in the atmosphere is 400 parts per million for the first time in recorded history. Four million years ago was the last time planet earth has had that high of concentration. Forest fires are becoming more intense as climate change is increasing to a greater degree the larger and more devastating high intensity fires. The Rim fire that burned 250,000 acres around Yosemite National Park and the Yarnell Hill fire around Prescott, Arizona killed nineteen fire fighters during the devastation.

In 2014 President Obama announced rules to cut carbon pollution from power plants. These plants are the largest contributor to greenhouse gas emissions. The multinational companies of Asia Pulp and Paper and Unilever pledge to cut deforestation in half by 2020 and eliminate it by 2030 as a result of the United Nations Climate Summit. The Paris Climate Agreement of 2015 set a 1.5 degree warning goal. In 2015 Republicans declared their intention to pass bills to force approval of the Keystone XL pipeline. It would bring extensive amounts of tar sands oil from Canada to the Gulf Coast for refining and shipping. Environmental health consequences of the pipeline are neglected by the Republican decision.

There is more evidence in 2016 that shows environmental pollution and desecration has negative health consequences. All life forms on earth suffers from extreme weather events, all types of pollution, and a wide range of diseases. In 2016 temperatures on earth were 1.1 degree higher than the pre-industrial average which is very close to the 1.5 degree warning goal of the Paris Climate Agreement of 2015. In 2016 the top environmental issues are overpopulation, pollution, deforestation, urban sprawl, loss of biodiversity, waste disposal, and water pollution. The year 2016 was the third year in a row to be hotter than all other years before. Also, of the seventeen hottest years on record, sixteen of them have occurred since 2000.

In 2017 Donald J. Trump becomes the most anti-environmental American president in history supplanting George W. Bush. President Trump begins to launch an all-out assault on environmental science; appoint corrupt industry people to positions of high public responsibility; and will attempt to dismantle regulations that protect public health and natural resources. President Trump withdraws the United States from the Paris Climate agreement, further isolating the United States from global environmental protection. The rise in global sea levels is accelerating and is now at 3.3 millimeters annually. President Trump plans to trim two million acres from Utah national monuments to allow mineral and petroleum exploitation. The year 2017 becomes the second hottest year on record just behind 2016.

The Camp Fire destroyed the entire community in Paradise, California, where 27,000 people lived. The nearby towns of Concow and Maglia were also mostly destroyed. The fire destroyed about 19,000 buildings and killed around 86 people. The Camp Fire was the deadliest fire in California history and the deadliest and most destructive in the United States since 1918. The conditions of the area were severe with dry weather for seven months, drought conditions for years, heavy grass, low humidity because of wind, high winds, and very dry fuel for the fire conditions. Brush piles left over from past logging events and continual encroaching of human population and home building in wildland-urban areas were factors that helped spread the devastation. Air pollution from the fire spread to the areas of San Francisco and Central Valley causing severe health problems for many individuals. Mental health issues exploded with survival guilt, post-traumatic stress disorder, anxiety, depression, suicidal thoughts, and relationship issues. The displacement and economic impact were devastating to the area of the Camp Fire and far beyond. After 200 days of drought conditions related to climate change the area was primed for a catastrophic environmental occurrence.

In 2018 the British medical journal Lancet reports that pollution is among the most serious worldwide health problems. Fourteen states sue the United States EPA over delays in methane emissions regulations. The Trump administration eases Obama-era standard on the disposal of toxic coal ash for coal fired power plants. The Intergovernmental Panel on Climate Change (IPCC) report says that if the global temperature rises by 1.5 degrees C, humans will face unprecedented climate related risks and weather events. The report says that the world is on track for a 3-4 degree temperature rise. The report also says that this is the final call and that this is the most extensive warning thus far on the risks of rising global temperatures. The United States and three other oil producing countries rejects the Climate change report of IPCC. The Trump administration ends 2018 by trying to roll back water protection. In 2018 carbon emissions rose by 3.4%. This is the second largest gain in twenty years. Transportation is the largest area if carbon emissions because of jet fuel and diesel fuel. Gasoline carbon emissions had a slight decrease. Also, in 2018, the Western Monarch Butterfly declined about 86% according to the Xerces Society which is an international nonprofit organization. Habitat destruction and droughts caused by climate change. On the coast of California the Monarch Butterfly population decreased from 148,000 in 2017 to 20,456 in 2018. Scientists predict that the Monarch Butterfly may be extinct by 2038.

Knowing... and being tenants of planet earth. There is a duty to warn and to protect. In the field of mental health practice there is a "duty to warn" in which a professional must contact a person if a client says they want to harm that person. Or, if a client says she or he wants to do harm to her or himself the professional must contact the authorities. Extending that to the level of all living things humanity has a duty to warn and protect itself and all of the living environment. This mandate applies to each individual, each community, each business, each church, each social and spiritual group, each corporation, each county, each state, and each nation. The early naturalists followed the "duty to warn and protect" mandate. The last fifty years, as stated earlier, gave warnings and asked for the need to protect all living things. The last fifty years also gave us many examples of the continual exploitation and degradation of life on earth, including humanity. Who speaks for the living? Humankind!

EARLY NATURALISTS TRANSFORMATIONAL VOICES

It seems right at this point that the early naturalists are heard from again. Their words and quotes are timeless. They knew things during their time on planet earth, thoughts, feelings, ideas, beliefs, that they felt necessary to share in their personal and public words and writings. They were not the first to speak for the natural world, but they each left a transformational gift that invites human beings to develop an earth conscience. It is a sacred calling. Humanity must choose either the path of loss, devastation, and extreme grief or the path of joining and partnering with all living things as an equal, fellow traveler to healing in the life-giving world.

"In my deepest troubles, I frequently would wrench myself from the persons around me and retire to some secluded part of our noble forests." John James Audubon

"It's not what you look at that matters, it's what you see. Nature will bear the closest inspection. She invites us to lay our eye level with her smallest leaf, and take an insect view of its plain." Henry David Thoreau

"Years of drought and famine come and years of flood and famine come, and the climate is not changed with dance, libation or prayer." John Wesley Powell

"When we try to pick out anything by itself, we find it hitched to everything else in the universe." John Muir

"The vast possibilities of our great future will become realities only if we make ourselves responsible for that future." Gifford Pinchot

"The forests are the flags of nature. They appeal to all and awaken inspiring universal feelings. Enter the forest and the boundaries of nations are forgotten. It may be that some time an immortal pine will be the flag of a united peaceful world." Enos Mills

"A thing is right when it tends to preserve the integrity, stability and beauty of the biotic community. It is wrong when it tends otherwise." Aldo Leopold

"The more clearly we can focus our attention on the wonders and realities of the universe about us, the less taste we shall have for destruction". Rachel Carson

RESOURCES

Part I: Naturalist's Voices From the Past

1. Audubon, John James. <u>Audubon by Himself.</u> Edited by Alice Ford. Garden City, N.Y.: The Natural History Press, 1969.
2. <u>Audubon's America.</u> Edited by Donald C. Peatts. Boston: Houghton Mifflin Co., 1940.
3. <u>Delineations of American Scenery and Character.</u> London: Simpkin, Marshall, Hamilton, Kent and Co., 1926.
4. <u>Letters of John James Audubon.</u> Edited by Howard C. Corning. Boston: The Club of Odd Volumes, 1930.
5. Audubon, Lucy G. <u>The Life of John James Audubon, the Naturalist.</u> New York: G. P. Putnam and Son, 1869.
6. Audubon, Maria R. <u>Audubon and His Journals.</u> New York: Charles Scribner's Sons, 1897.
7. Burroughs, John. <u>John James Audubon.</u> Boston: George H. Ellis Co., 1902.
8. Ford, Alice. <u>John James Audubon.</u> Norman, Okla.: The University of Oklahoma Press, 1964.
9. McDermott, John Francis. <u>Audubon the Naturalist.</u> New York: D. Appleton and Co., 1917.
10. St. John, Mrs. Horace. <u>Life of Audubon. The Naturalist of the New World.</u> Philadelphia: J. B. Lippincott Co., 1918.
11. McDermott, John Francis. <u>Audubon the Naturalist.</u> New York: D. Appleton and Co., 1917.
12. Thoreau, Henry David. <u>Faith in a Seed</u>. Island Press. Washington, D.C., 1993
13. <u>Thoreau, Henry David</u>. 2 vols. Edited by Bradford Torrey and Francis H. Allen. Dover Publications. New York: NY1962.
14. <u>Letters to Various Persons</u>. Edited by Ralph Waldo Emerson. Boston, 1865.
15. Thoreau, Henry David. <u>The Maine Woods</u>. Harper and Row. New York: NY. 1987.
16. Thoreau, Henry David. <u>Natural History Essays</u>. Gibbs Smith. Salt Lake City, UT. 1988.

17. Thoreau, Henry David. Reform Papers. Edited by Wendell Glick. Princeton University Press. Princeton, NJ. 1973

18. Thoreau, Henry David. Walden and Civil Disobedience. Signet Publishers. New York, NY. 1986

19. Thoreau, Henry David. A week, Walden The Maine Woods, Cape Cod. Library of America. New York: NY. 1985.

20. Reflections at Walden Hallmark Cards, Inc. Kansas City: MO. 1971.

21. Thoreau, Henry David. A Week on the Concord and Merrimack Rivers / Walden; Or, Life in the Woods / The Maine Woods / Cape Cod. Library of America. New York: NY. 1985.

22. Powell, John Wesley. Contributions to North American Ethnology. Vol. I-VII. Washington, D.C.: Government Printing Office, 1877-1893.

23. Powell, John Wesley. Down the Colorado. New York: E. P. Dutton, 1969. Powell, John Wesley.

24. Report on the Lands of the Arid Region of the United States. Washington, D.C.: Government Printing Office, 1878.

25. Selected Prose of John Wesley Powell. Edited by George Crossette. Boston: David R. Godine, 1970.

26. Powell, John Wesley. The Exploration of the Colorado River. Chicago: The University of Chicago Press, 1957.

27. U.S. Geographical and Geological Survey of the Rocky Mountain Region. Washington, D.C.: Government Printing Office, 1879.

28. Terrell, John Upton. The Man Who Rediscovered America. New York: Weybright and Talley, 1969.

29. Hawthorne, Hildegarde, and Mills, Esther Burnell. Enos Mills of the Rockies. Boston: Houghton Mifflin Co., 1935.

30. Muir, John. A Thousand Mile Walk to the Gulf. Boston: Houghton Mifflin Co., 1913.

31. Muir, John. My First Summer in the Sierra. Boston: Houghton Mifflin Co., 1911.

32. Muir, John. Our National Parks. Boston: Houghton Mifflin Co., 1901.

33. Muir, John. Steep Trails, Boston: Houghton Mifflin Co., 1918.

34. The Life and Letters of John Muir. Edited by William F. Babb. Boston: Houghton Mifflin Co., 1923.

35. Muir, John. The Mountains of California. New York: The Century Co., 1894.

36. Muir, John. The Story of My Boyhood and Youth. Boston: Houghton Mifflin Co., 1917.

37. Muir, John. Travels to Alaska. Boston: Houghton Mifflin Co., 1915.

38. Peattie, Donald C. Singing in the Wilderness A Salute to John James Audubon. New York: G. P. Putnam's Sons, 1925.

39. Pinchot, Gifford. Breaking New Ground. New York: Harcourt, Brace and Co., 1947.

40. Pinchot, Gifford. Use of the National Forests. Washington, D.C.: United States Department of Agriculture, 1907.

41. Pinchot, Gifford, and Graves, Harry. The White Pine. Washington, D.C.: United States Department of Agriculture, 1896.

42. Pinkett, Harold T. Gifford Pinchot. Private and Public Forester. Chicago: University of Illinois Press, 1968.

43. McGeary, M. Nelson. Gifford Pinchot. Princeton, N.J.: Princeton University Press, 1960.

44. Mills, Enos A. Enos A. Mills Author, Sneaker, Nature Guide. Longs Peak, Colo.: The Trail Book Store, 1917.

45. Mills, Enos. Romance of Geology. Boston: Houghton Mifflin Co., 1932.

46. Mills, Enos. The Adventures of a Nature Guide. Garden City, N.Y.: Doubleday, Page and Co., 1920.

47. Mills, Enos. The Spell of the Rockies. Boston: Houghton Mifflin Co., 1911.

48. The Story of Estes Park, Grand Lake, and the Rocky Mountain National Park. Longs Peak, Colo.: The Trail Bookstore, 1917.

49. Mills, Enos. Waiting in the Wilderness. Garden City, N.Y.: Doubleday, Page and Co., 1921.

50. Mills, Enos. Wildlife on the Rockies. Boston: Houghton Mifflin Co., 1909.

51. The Sand Country of Aldo Leopold. San Francisco: The Sierra Club, 1973.

52. Leopold, Aldo. A Sand County Almanac. New York: Oxford University Press, 194

53. Leopold, Aldo. Round River. New York: Oxford University Press, 1953.

54. Leopold, Aldo. Game Management. New York: Charles Scribner's Sons, 1939

55. Carson, Rachel. Silent Spring. New York: Houghton Mifflin, 1962.
56. Carson, Rachel. The Sea Around Us. Oxford: Oxford University Press. 1951
57. Carson, Rachel. The Edge of the Sea. New York: Houghton Mifflin, 1953
58. Carson, Rachel. Under the Sea-Wind. New York: Simon and Schuster. 1941
59. Rachel Carson's Biography. Retrieved October 10, 2017 from http://www.rachelcarson.org/Bio.aspx
60. Lear, Linda. Rachel Carson: Witness for Nature. New York: NY. Henry Holt and Company. 1997.
61. Udall, Stewart L. The Quiet Crisis. New York: Holt, Rinehart and Winston, 1963.

Part II: Environmental Degradation

1. *Environmental Degradation Facts*. The World Counts, April 24, 2014. Retrieved October, 6, 2017 from World Counts. http://www.theworldcounts.com/stories/environmental-degradation-facts
2. James, Ian and Reilly, Steve. *Pumped beyond limits, many U.S aquifers in decline*. The Desert Sun. Retrieved February 7, 2017 from Desert Sun. https://www.desertsun.com/story/news/environment/2015/12/10/pumped-beyond-limits- many-us-aquifers-decline/76570380/
3. Finley, Bruce. *Similar toxic chemicals found in food packaging*. Denver Post, Feb. 1, 2017.
4. Finley, Bruce. *How dirty is it: City wrestles with pollution from central coal-fired power plant*. Denver Post Jan. 15, 2017.
5. *Our Nation's air: Status and trends through 2008*. US Environmental Protection Agency (EPA) Office of Air Quality Planning and Standards. Washington D.C.: EPA 2010.
6. Avramova, Nana. *Climate change is already here and heat waves are having the biggest effect*. CNN. November 28, 2018. Retrieved from

CNN December 5, 2018.
http://www.cnn.com/2018/11/28/health/global-climate-change-and-health- report-intl/index.html

7. Miller, Brandon. *The past four years have been the hottest on record and we are seeing the effects*. November 30, 2018. Retrieved from CNN December 11, 2018.
    https://www.cnn.com/2018/11/29/world/climate-change-wmo-2018-report-wxc/index.html

8. Tutton, Mark. *Carbon emissions to hit all-time high*. CNN. December 5, 2018. Retrieved December 14, 2018.
    http://www.cnn.com/2018/12/05/world/emissions-lglobal-carbon-budget/index.html?no-st=1544466908

9. Harris, Amy. *Natural Changes that Can Effect an Ecosystem*. Sciencing. March 13, 2018. Retrieved from Sciencing May 23, 2018.
    https://sciencing.com/natural-changes-can-affect-ecosystem-6777.html

10. Foxworth, Miles. *U.S. Schools Struggle to Maintain a Healthy Learning Environment*. Oct. 1, 2017. Retrieved from Healthy School Environment May 15, 2018.
    https://webspm.com/articles/2017/10/01/healthy-learning-environment.aspx?m=1

11. Miller, Brandon. *2016 was the hottest year on record—again*. CNN Meteorologist. January 18, 2017. Retrieved from CNN June 17, 2018.
    https://www.cnn.com/2017/01/18/world/2016-hottest-year/index.html

12. Christensen, Jen. *16,000 Scientists sign dire warning to humanity over health of planet*. November 15, 2017. CNN. Retrieved from CNN January 14, 2018.
    https://www.cnn.com/2017/11/14/health/scientists-worn-humanity/index.html

13. Motkar, Snehal. *Causes and Effects of Desertification We Should Be concerned About.* Help Save Nature. February 24, 2018. Retrieved from Help Save Nature June 6, 2018.
    https://helpsavenature.com/what-is-environmental-

ethics.amp"Environmental Degradation Facts." The World Counts, April 24, 2014. Retrieved October, 6, 2017 from World Counts. http://www.theworldcounts.com/stories/environmental-degradation-facts

14. *Concern Energy Future: Be Green. Stay Green.* Renewable Resources Coalition. December 4, 2016. Retrieved March 12, 2017 from Renewable Resources coalition. https://www.conserve-energy-future.com/15-current-environmental-problems.php

15. Vijayalaxmi Kinhal. *Love to Know.* Green Living. Retrieved from Green Living July 9, 2017. https://greenliving.lovetoknow.com/Top_30_Environmental_Concerns

Part III: Environmental Impact: Body, Mind and Spirit

Environmental Distress and Physical Health

1. World Health Organization (WHO). *Preventing disease through healthy environments.* Geneva, Switzerland: WHO; 2006.

2. Patz J, Campbell-Lendrum D, Holloway T, et. Al. *Impact of regional climate change on human health.* Nature. 2005 Nov. 17; 438(7066):310-7.

3. Kinney PL. *Climate change, air quality, and human health.* American Journal of Preventive Medicine. 2008 Nov; 35(5):459-67

4. Srinivasan S, O'Fallon LR, Dearry A. *Creating Health communities, health homes, health people: Initiating a research agenda on the built environment and public health.* American Journal of Public Health. 2003 Sep; 93(9):1446-50

5. Canadian Environmental Protection Act: Health Canada and Environment Canada. *Environment and Climate: Pollution and Waste.* May 29, 2017. Retrieved January 24, 2018, from http://www.hc.se.ge.ca/english/iyh/environment//cepa_overview.html

6. Government of Canada. *Protecting your Health and the Environment*. September 30, 2016. Retrieved February 7, 2018 from https://www.canada.ca/en/health-canada/services/consumer-product-safety/pesticides-pest-management/public/protecting-your-health-enviro

7. McMichael A.J., Campbell-Lendrum D.H., Corvalan C.F., Ebi K.L., Githeko A., Scheraga J.D. Woodward A. *Climate change and human health-risks and responses*. World Health Organization. 2003, P. 250. Retrieved February 16, 2018 from http://ww.who.int/globalchange/publications/cchhbook/en/

8. *Water for Health-Taking Charge*. Report, World Health Organization. 2001. Retrieved March 2, 2018, from http://wwwwho.int/water_sanitation_health/takingcharge/en/

9. *Ecohealth: Improving the Health of People and the Environment*. International Development Resource Center. October 27, 2010. Retrieved from International Development Resource Center, June 27, 2016. https://www.idrc.ca/en/article/ecohealth-improving-health-people-and-environment

10. Resnik, David B. and Portier, Christopher J. *Environment and Health*. From Birth to Death and Bench to Clinic: The Hastings Center Bioethics Briefing Book for Journalists, Policymakers, and Campaigns, ed. Mary Crowley (Garrison, NY: The Hasting Center, 2008), 59-62.

11. Holldren, John P. *Science and Technology for Sustainable Well-Being*. Science, January, 2008.

12. McMichael, Anthony J., Powles, John, Butler, Colin D. and Uauy, Ricardo. *Food, Livestock Production, Energy, Climate Change, and Health*. The Lancet, October 2007.

13. *Understanding the Science That Shows the Environment Affecting Human Health*. 2010. Retrieved from Sustainable Baby Steps June 24, 2016. http://www.sustainablebabysteps.com/environment-affecting-human-health.html

14. *United Nations Environment Programme - UN Environment Document*. Oct. 11, 1991. Retrieved from United Nations

Environment Programme, PDF. May 13, 2016
https://wedocs.unep.org/rest/bitstreams/2261/retrieve.

15. *Climate and Health*. Centers for Disease Control. Retrieved from
Centers for Disease Control November 18, 2018.
https://www.cdc.gov/climateandhealth/default.htm

16. Yassi, Annalee and Kjellström, Tord. *Linkages Between
Environmental and Occupational Health.* May 9, 2011. Retrieved
from Encyclopedia of Occupational Health and Safety April 7, 2016.
http://www.iloencyclopaedia.org/component/k2/88-53-
environmental-health-hazards/linkages-between-environmental-
and-occupational-health

17. *Vector Born Diseases*. World Health Organization. May 30, 2017.
Retrieved from WHO February 24, 2018. https://www.who.int/news-
room/fact-sheets/detail/vector-borne-diseases

18. Meyer, Robinson. *New, Major Evidence That Fracking Harms Human
Health*. Dec 13, 2017, The Atlantic. Retrieved from The Atlantic March
23, 2018.
https://www.theatlantic.com/amp/article/548315/

19. *Food and Waterborne Diarrheal Disease*. Centers for Disease
Control and Prevention. December 11, 2014. Retrieved from CDC
September 25, 2016.
https://www.cdc.gov/climateandhealth/effects/food_waterborne.h
tm

Environmental Distress and Mental Health

1. *Diagnostic Statistical Manual*. Psychiatric Association. American
Psychiatric Publishing. Washington, D.C.: 2013.

2. Evans, GW and Urban J. *The built environment and mental health*.
Health 2003. Retrieved from Health April 19, 2017.
https://www.ncbi.nlm.nih.gov/pubmed/14709704

3. Peters, Shannon. *Connections Between Climate Change Concerns,
Mental Health, and Pro-Environmental Actions*. Science, Psychiatry,
and Social Justice.

4. January 25, 2018. Retrieved from Science, Psychiatry, and Social Justice May 2, 2018. https://www.madinamerica.com/2018/01/connections-climate-change-concerns-mental-health-pro-environmental-actions/

5. Jordan, Rob. *Stanford researchers find mental health prescription: Nature.* Stanford Woods Institute for the Environment. June 30, 2015. Retrieved from Stanford News July 9, 2016. https://news.stanford.edu/2015/06/30/hiking-mental-health-063015/

6. Tobin, Danielle, Avison, William, Gilliland, Jason. *Mental health benefits of interactions with nature in children and teenagers: a systematic review.* Journal of Epidemiology and Community Health. Volume 72, Issue 10. Retrieved from Journal of Epidemiology and Community Health October 18, 2018. https://jech.bmj.com/content/72/10/958

7. Jones, Lucy. *How Nature Benefits your Mental Health.* Tonic. May 24, 2016. Retrieved from Tonic April 29, 2017. https://tonic.vice.com/en_us/article/av37kp/how-nature-benefits-your-mental-health

8. *Mood Walks for Older Adults: An Ontario Pilot Project.* Mood Walks. 2014. Retrieved from Mood Walks August 4, 2017. https://www.moodwalks.ca/about-mood-walks/evaluation-summary-report/

9. *The Nurture of Nature: Natural Settings and Their Mental Health Benefits.* Mood Walks, March, 2013. Retrieved from Mood Walks May 30, 2016. https://www.moodwalks.ca/about-mood-walks/the-nurture-of-nature-natural-settings-and-their-mental-health-benefits/

10. LaBier, Douglas, Ph.D. *Why Connecting With Nature Elevates Your Mental Health.* The New Resilience. Jan. 8, 2018. Retrieved from Psychology Today. March 14, 2018. https://www.psychologytoday.com/us/blog/the-new-resilience/201801/why-connecting-nature-elevates-your-mental-health

11. Bratman, GN, Hamilton, JP, Daily, GC. *The Impacts of Nature Experience on Human Cognitive Function*. The New York Academy of Sciences. February, 2012. Retrieved from The New York Academy of Sciences August 19, 2017.
https://www.ncbi.nlm.nih.gov/pubmed/22320203

12. Pearson, David G. and Craig. Tony. *The great outdoors? Exploring the mental health benefits of natural environments*. Frontiers in Psychology, Oct. 21, 2014. Retrieved from Frontiers in Psychology June 1, 2017.
https://www.ncbi.nlm.nih.gov/pmc/articles/PMC4204431/

13. Mantler, Annemarie and Logan, Alan C. *Natural Environments and Mental Health*. Advances in Integrative Medicine. April 15, 2015. Retrieved from Advances in Integrative Medicine September 9, 2017.
https://www.sciencedirect.com/science/article/pii/S2212962615000371

14. Schmidt, Charles W. *Environmental Connections: A Deeper Look into Mental Illness*. Environmental Health Perspectives. August, 2007. Retrieved from Environmental Health Perspectives January 23, 2018.
https://www.ncbi.nlm.nih.gov/pmc/articles/PMC1940091/

15. *How the Environment Affects mental health.* Cambridge University Press. January, 2005. Retrieved from Cambridge University Press April 18, 2017. https://www.cambridge.org/core/journals/the-british-journal-of-psychiatry/article/how-the-environment-affects-mental-health/9CDA36F86AB77783F88F9B76D03FD69F

Environmental Distress and Spiritual Health

1. Tucker, Evelyn and Grim, John. *Overview of World Religions and Ecology*. Yale University. 2009. Retrieved March 14, 2017. Columbia University Press.
http://fore.yale.edu/files/Forum_History.pdf

2. Steven Jeffrey. *Spirituality and Environment*. August, 2003. Retrieved from Gatherings: Seeking Ecopsychology, September 23, 2017.

https://www.ecopsychology.org/journal/gatherings8/html/spirit/spirituality-jeffrey.html

3. *Interconnectedness of Environment and Spirituality*. Environmental Spirituality. September 28, 2010. Retrieved from Environmental Spirituality, July 15, 2016.
https://www.jpic-assumpta.org/012-the-interconnectedness-of

4. Maathai, Wangari. *Spiritual Environmentalism: Healing Ourselves by Replenishing the Earth*. May 25, 2011. Retrieved from Replenishing the Earth: Spiritual Values for Healing Ourselves and the World (Doubleday Religion). December 11, 2017.
https://www.huffingtonpost.com/wangari-maathai/spiritual-environmentalis_b_762801.html

5. *Religion and environmentalism*. Retrieved from Wikipedia July 28, 2016.
https://en.wikipedia.org/wiki/Religion_and_environmentalism

6. Grim, John A. *Indigenous Traditions and Ecology*. July 15, 2001.Yale University. Retrieved from Religions of the World, August 2, 2016.
http://www.hup.harvard.edu/catalog.php?isbn=9780945454281

7. Denny, Frederick M. *Islam and Ecology: A Bestowed Trust Inviting Balanced Stewards.* University of Colorado. Retrieved from The Forum on Religion and Ecology at Yale University, February 18, 2017.
http://fore.yale.edu/religion/islam/

8. Chapple, Christopher Key. *Hinduism Jainism and Ecology*. Loyola Marymount University. Published in Earth Ethics 10, no. 1. Fall 1998.

9. Tucker, Mary Evelyn. *Confucianism and Ecology: Potential and Limits*. Yale University. September 15, 2009. Retrieved from Patheos June 6, 2017. http://www.patheos.com/Resources/Additional-Resources/confucianism-and-Ecology.html

10. Bohannon, Richard. Religions and Environments. Bloombury. New York 2014

Part IV: Into the Future: Is it the End or Is it the Beginning?

1. Jaafari, Joseph Darius. *Saving the Earth by Dying*. Nation Swell. February 20, 2018. Retrieved from Nation Swell November 18, 2018. http://nationalswell.com/green-burials-save-earth-dying/amp/
2. *We can save the Earth. Here's how*. World Economic Forum. September 21, 2018. Retrieved from World Economic Forum, October 19, 2018. https://www.weforum.org/agenda/2018/09/we-can-save-the-earth-heres-how/
3. *Our Planet is at breaking point. But it's not too late to save it*. World Economic Forum. January 5, 2017. Retrieved from World Economic Forum, September 28, 2017. https://www.weforum.org/agenda/2017/01/our-planet-is-at-breaking-point-but-it-s-not-toolate-to-save-it
4. *How Environmental Technology is Helping the Earth*. Digital Care. May 19, 2017. Retrieved from Digital Care, December 4, 2017. https://www.digitalcare.org/environmental-technology-is-helping-the-earth/
5. *Technology can help us save the planet. But more than anything, we must learn to value nature*. World Economic Forum. August 23, 2018. Retrieved from World Economic Forum, November 19, 2018. https://www.weforum.org/agenda/2018/08/here-s-how-technology-can-help-us-save-the-planet/
6. Alexander, Samuel, Gleeson, Brendan. *The Suburbs are the spiritual home of overconsumption. But they also hold the key to a better future*. December. 13, 2018. Retrieved from The Conversation, December 29, 2018. http://theconversation.com/the-suburbs-are-the-spiritual-home-of-overconsumption-but-they-also-hold-the-key-to-a-better-future-108496
7. Daley, John. *As Colorado Looks to Renewables, Industries Like Health Care Want to Go Green Too*. Colorado Public Radio. December 8, 2016. Retrieved from Colorado Public Radio, March 19, 2017. http://www.cpr.org/news/story/as-colorado-looks-to-renewables-industries-like-health-care-want-to-go-green-too

8. Nesbit, Jeff. *3 things businesses can do to win the climate change fight.* CNN. Nov. 15, 2018. Retrieved from CNN, December 1, 2018. https://www.cnn.com/2018/11/15/perspectives/un-climate-change-report-businesses/index.html

9. Eisenstein, Charles. <u>Climate</u>. North Atlantic Books. Berkeley, CA: 2018

10. Brown, Lester R. <u>The Twenty Ninth Day.</u> Worldwatch Institute. WW Norton and Co. New York: NY. 1978

11. Brown, Lester R. <u>Eco-Economy</u>. Earth Policy Institute. W.W. Norton and Co. New York: NY. 2001

12. *Environmental History Timeline.* Retrieved from Environmental History Timeline. October 19, 2018. http://environmentalhistory.org/20th-century/

13. *Environmental History Timeline.* Retrieved from Environmental History Timeline. October 20, 2018. http://environmentalhistory.org/21st-century/

Knowing: Only Tenants of Planet Earth

1. Abbey, Edward. *Beyond the Wall: Essays from the Outside.* Macmillan. NY. 1984

2. Berry, Thomas. *The Spirituality of the Earth.* 1990. Liberating Life: Contemporary Approaches in Ecological Theology. Charles Birch, William Eaken and Jay B. McDaniel. Otis Books. Maryknoll, NY: 1990

3. Louv, Richard. <u>Last Child in the Woods.</u> Algonquin Books. Chapel Hill: NC. 2008

4. Louv, Richard. <u>The Nature Principle</u>. Algonquin Books. Chapel Hill: NC. 2011.

5. Berry Wendell. <u>Our Only World</u>. Counterpoint. Berkeley: CA. 2015

6. Berry, Thomas. <u>The Sacred Universe</u>. Columbia University Press. New York: NY. 20

About the Author:

Dr. Laren R. Winter lives with his wife, Karen, in Colorado where he enjoys hiking and biking in the Rocky Mountains. He has a doctorate degree in education with an emphasis in Outdoor Environmental Education and Psychology. Laren is a retired college professor in School Psychology and is a Licensed School Psychologist and Licensed Marriage and Family Therapist. His other published book is *The Einstein Posse* a fictional book about a school psychologist in a Colorado mountain community.

www.ingramcontent.com/pod-product-compliance
Lightning Source LLC
Chambersburg PA
CBHW051347280526
45784CB00007B/2852